A Practical Guide to Azure DevOps

Learn by doing

Third Edition

Milindanath Hewage

Contents

Contents

Acknowledgements

I would like to thank my wife, Viveka for being so patient during my busy days writing this book. This book would not have been a reality without my parents who brought me up to this level. So, my wishes go to them for a long and a happy life ahead.

I would also like to thank both Vindya & Viveka for proofreading the content of the book. Finally, I would like to thank you who have spent time and money to buy this book and I hope it will be a useful tool in your Azure DevOps journey.

Introduction

DevOps has been a major topic among developers, testers, project managers and many others involved in building software products nowadays. The general term *DevOps* is basically the combination of Development(Dev) and Operations(Ops). However, there are many definitions of DevOps. Microsoft defines DevOps as

> *the union of **people**, **process**, and **technology** to continually provide value to customers[1]*

Azure DevOps has been created by Microsoft to achieve the core objectives of this definition.

There are many books written on the subject Azure DevOps. However, this book has taken a different approach. **Rather than going into details of so many technical information, this book mainly focuses on the practical aspect of Azure DevOps for beginners**. Therefore, you will see theoretical explanations only when needed to explain a certain scenario. I have tried my best to keep things very simple and always focus on completing a specific task using Azure DevOps.

In this edition, I focus on discussing the core features of Azure DevOps such as organization, projects, Azure Boards, Azure Repos and Azure Pipelines. As the Azure DevOps team regularly releases new updates to the product, I will try to update the book regularly to cover new topics in future editions of the book.

Introduction

Who this book is intended for?

This book is mainly intended for project managers, release managers, stakeholders and developers who are beginners to Azure DevOps and are not interested in reading detailed technical descriptions but rather would like to start things by doing. This will also help advanced users to understand some advanced concepts in a simple manner. Screenshots and images have been added as visual support for understanding each topic.

Requirements to run the examples.

All the examples used in this book are done using a PC with Windows 10 Pro operating system. Although it is not mandatory, it will be easy to follow along if you have a Windows PC. All the examples are done using Azure DevOps Services which is the cloud-based service for Azure DevOps.

Conventions used in this book

> 💡 Helpful tips will be shown like this

`programming codes and commands will be shown like this`

Your feedback on the book

As a reader of this book your feedback is very significant to improve the future versions of the book. So, please send your comments to milindanath@viminorge.com

Chapter 1
Creating an Azure DevOps Organization

What you will learn in this chapter

☑ Create new organization

☑ Microsoft or GitHub account

☑ Manage organization

☑ Project settings

☑ User management settings

☑ Billing

☑ Extensions

☑ Security policies

☑ Work item process settings

Creating a new organization is the first thing you must do to get started with Azure DevOps. For that, you have to have a Microsoft account. If you do not have one yet, you can create an account during the creation of your first organization.

Navigate to https://dev.azure.com. Here, you have two options to select. You can either click on the **Start free** button or if you already have a GitHub account you can click on the **Start free with GitHub** button. In this case, I am going to select the **Start free** button.

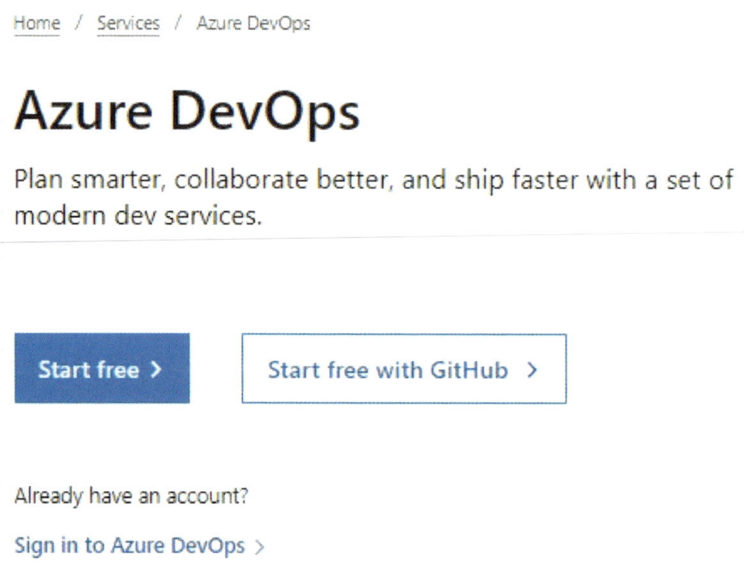

Figure 1: Azure DevOps Home Page

You will be redirected to the sign in page. If you do not have a Microsoft account, there is a possibility to create an account by clicking on the **Create one!** link.

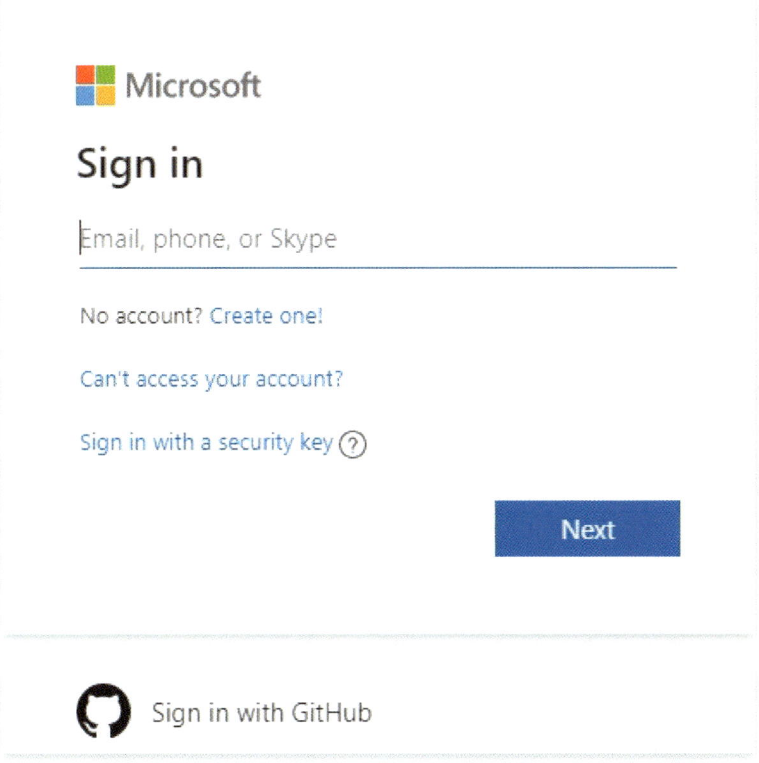

Figure 2: Sign into Microsoft account

Once you have successfully logged in, you can create your first project as shown in Figure 3.

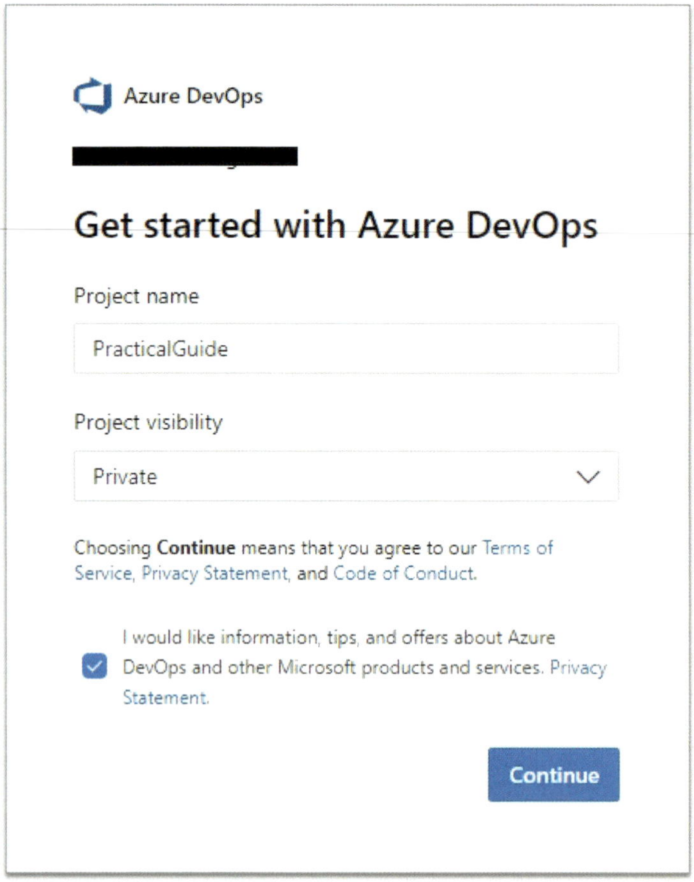

Figure 3: Create a project

Provide a name for your project and set the visibility according to your preference. You can select from **Private** or **Public**. Select **Public** if you want everyone in the public to interact with your project. Select **Private** if you want a closed-source project, where you and only those you give access to, can interact with the project. Once you have done all the necessary changes click on the **Continue** button.

A new organization will be created together with this new project. Now we are all set to start work in Azure DevOps. You have your first organization and the first project. However, the organization name might be selected randomly by Azure DevOps. Let us see how we can change the given organization name.

Navigate to the home page by clicking on the **Azure DevOps** logo. Now click on the **Organization settings** link on the bottom left hand corner.

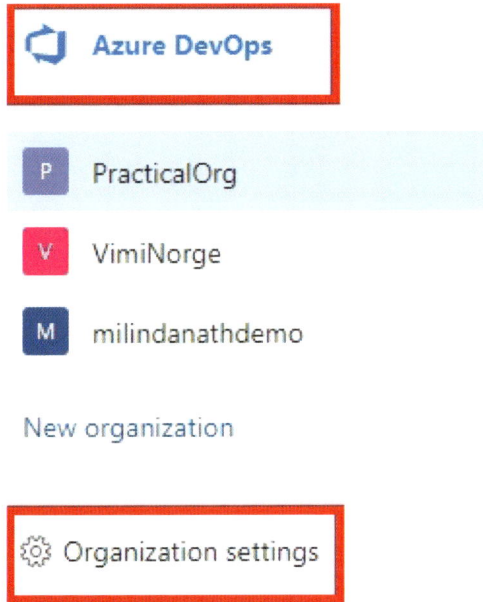

Figure 4: Azure DevOps logo & organization settings

You can change the name of your organization in the **Overview** section. Moreover, the owner of the Microsoft account who created the organization will be the owner of the organization. But if you want, you can transfer the ownership to someone else.

After you have done all these necessary changes to the new organization click on **Save**.

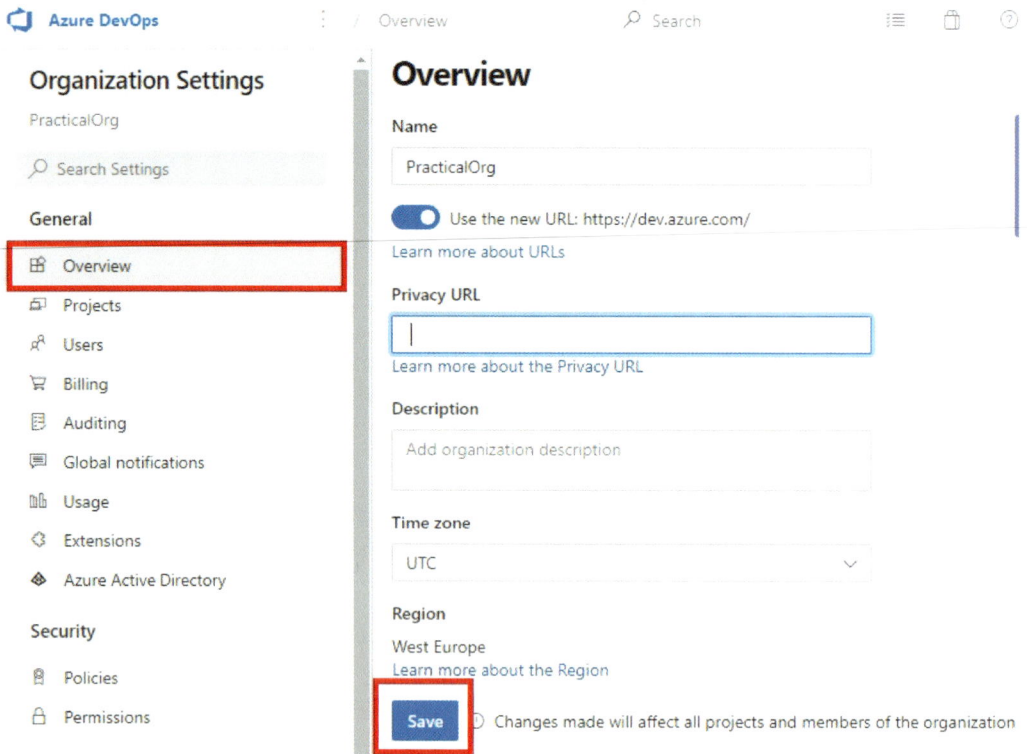

Figure 5: Organization Settings - General - Overview

You will see the following dialog box after clicking on the Save button. Accept the new changes by typing in your new organization name as shown in Figure 6.

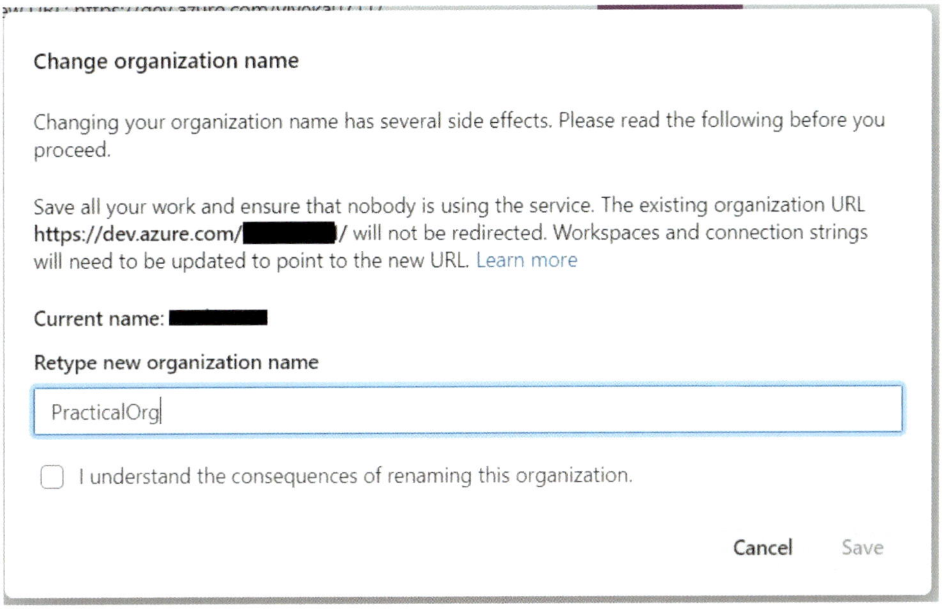

Figure 6: Change organization name

The new URL for your organization takes the form
https://dev.azure.com/{org.name}. For example, in this case it will be
https://dev.azure.com/practicalorg

Other organizational settings

There are number of settings that you can configure for your organization.
In this section, let us focus on some of the most important and most used
settings.

Projects

This section shows a list of all the projects associated with the selected
organization. In addition to that, you can create a new project, rename the
project, delete selected projects or search for existing projects in the
organization.

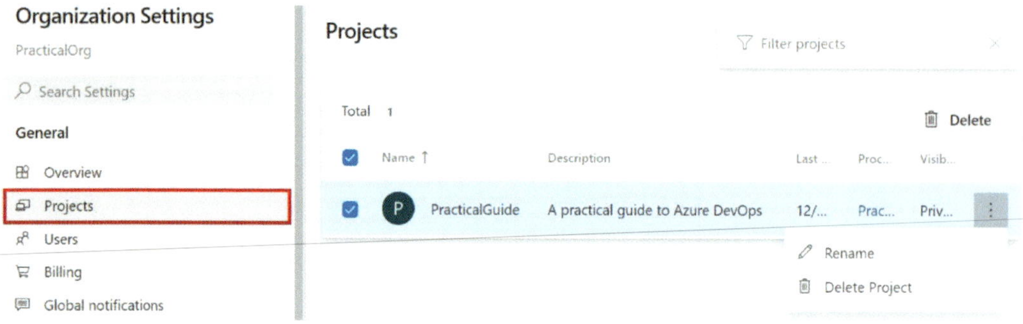

Figure 7: Projects Settings

Users

All the users added to the organization are displayed here.

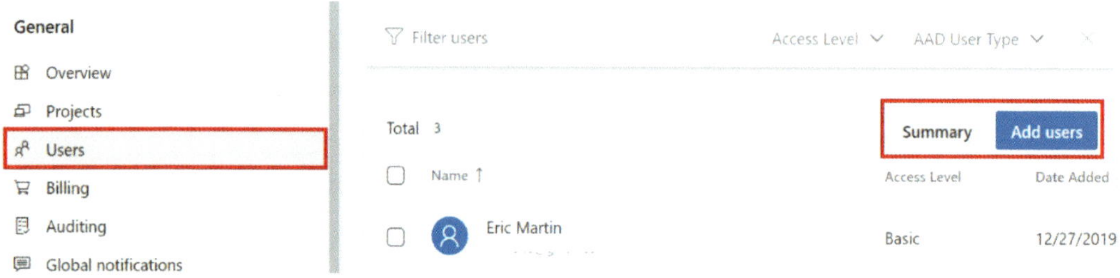

Figure 8: List of users connected to the organization

You can add new users to the organization by clicking on the **Add users** button. However, you need to have administrator rights to perform this type of operation.

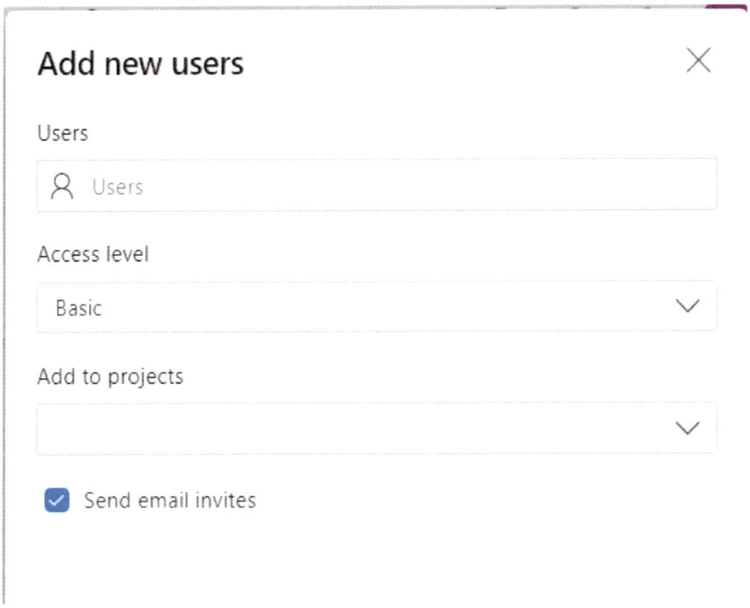

Figure 9: Add new users

First, type in the **email** of the person you want to add as a new user, and then select the user's **access level**. At the time of writing this book, for the free plan of Azure DevOps Services, you can add maximum of 5 free users under the access level **Basic**. Refer to section **Billing** for more information. In addition to that, you can specify on which projects, this user will be working on using the **Add to projects** dropdown. At the end, you can check **Send email invites** to notify the user about the invitation. Once the user has accepted the invitation, he/she will be added to the organization.

Billing

You can set up your billing information here. It is free for the first 5 Basic users. However, you have to setup billing if your team has more than 5 Basic users. You get 1800 (30 hours) free minutes of Microsoft Hosted CI/CD pipelines per month, and 1 Self-Hosted CI/CD. With this plan, you can only run one job at a time. In addition to that, you will get 2GB free storage for the Artifacts. You can find more information about pricing and subscriptions at https://docs.microsoft.com/en-us/azure/devops/organizations/billing/billing-faq?view=azure-devops&tabs=new-nav&viewFallbackFrom=vsts

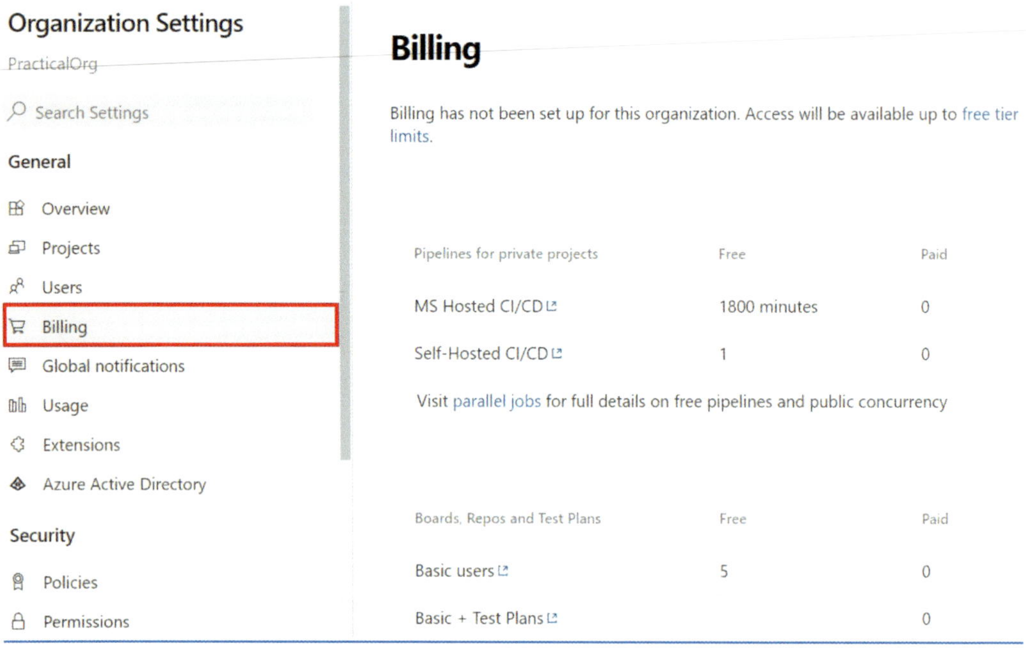

Figure 10: Billing settings under organization

Check Azure DevOps home page for latest information. At the moment the pricing information is located at https://azure.microsoft.com/en-us/pricing/details/devops/azure-devops-services/

Extensions

You can add extensions to your projects using the Azure DevOps marketplace. Click on the Browse marketplace button to see extensions available.

Organization Settings

PracticalOrg

🔍 Search Settings

General

🔲 Overview

🖳 Projects

👥 Users

🛒 Billing

🗩 Global notifications

📊 Usage

♻ Extensions

🔷 Azure Active Directory

Extensions   Security   Browse marketplace

Installed   Requested   Shared

No installed extensions were found matching your criteria.

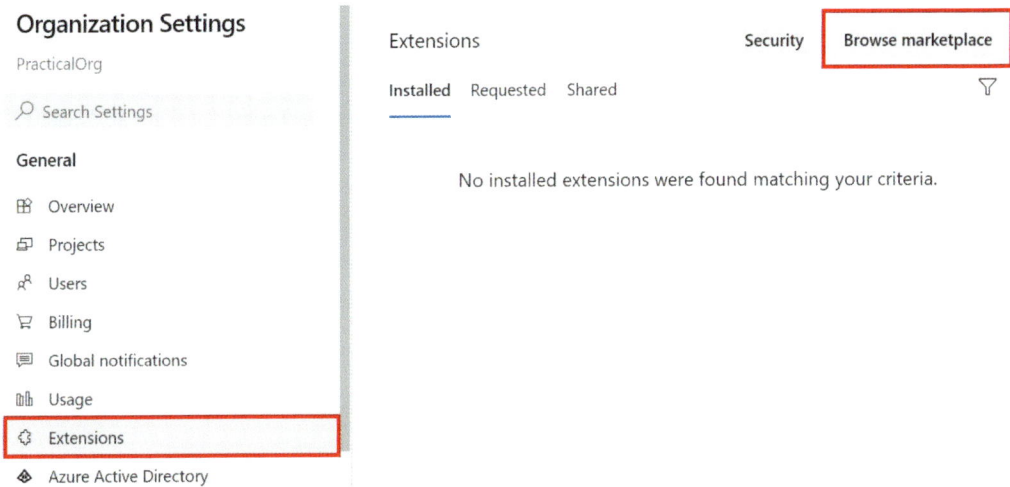

Figure 11: Install extensions at organization level

For example, if you want time tracking for your tasks you can get the extension "timetracker".

timesheet

3 Results   Showing: **All categories** ∨

Timesheet
CETAS INFORMAT   ⤓ 11
Use hot reload and debug directly in VS Code
★ ★ ★ ★ ★   FREE

Timetracker
7pace   ⤓ 12K
The complete solution to track and manage working time on work items.
★ ★ ★ ★ ★   FREE TRIAL

SSW TimePRO
SSW   ⤓ 1.1K
Stop wasting time entering timesheets, TimePRO lets you add your timesheets for the...
★ ★ ★ ★ ★   FREE

Figure 12: Azure DevOps marketplace

Security -> Policies

Here you can set up your policies with regards to security. For example, if your organization does not allow any public projects, then you can turn off **Allow public projects** option.

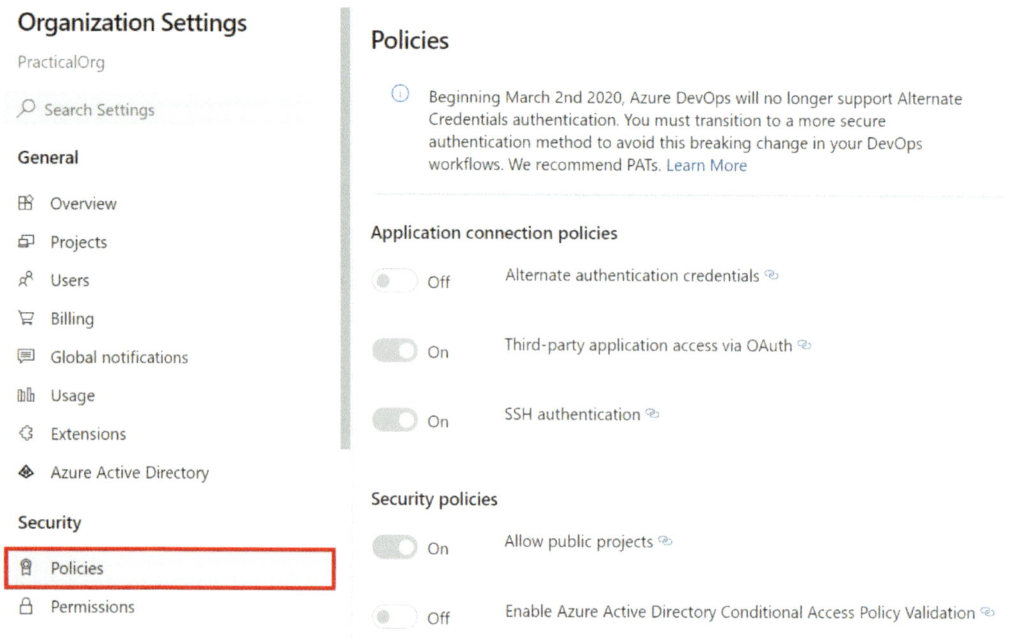

Figure 13: Security policies

Security -> Permissions

You can add groups to your organization and give them permission on different areas. For example, whether a group/user can create new projects or delete an existing project etc.

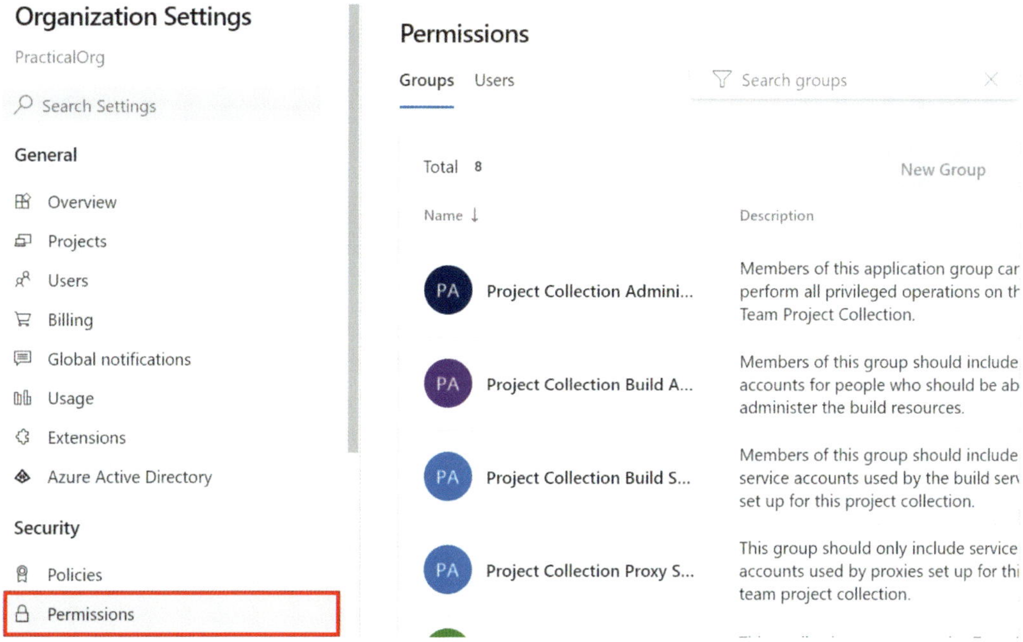

Figure 14: Security permissions

Boards - > Process

Here you can see the work item processes defined in Azure DevOps. You can customize these processes by creating inherited process if necessary. More information about these processes can be found in Chapter 2.

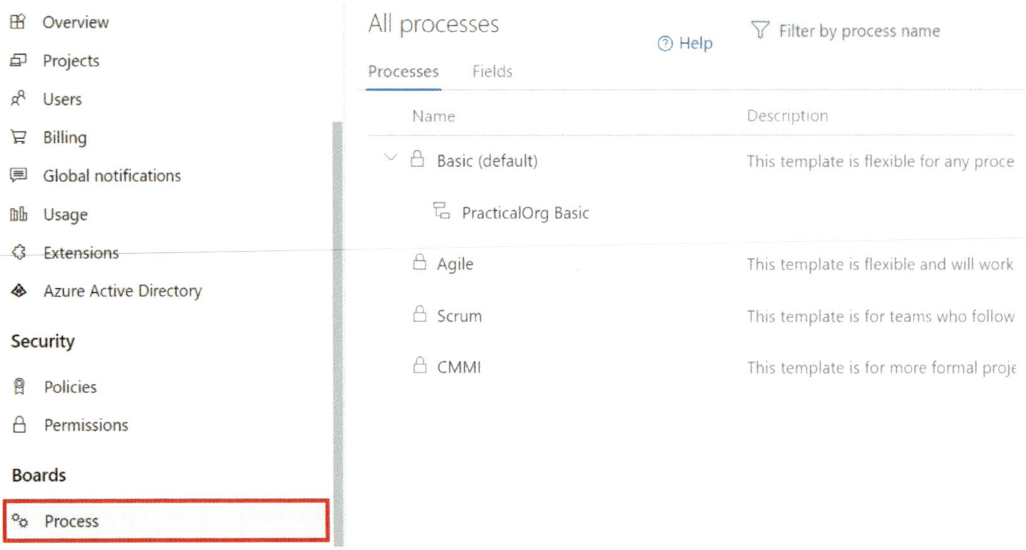

Figure 15: Work item process settings

Summary

In this chapter, we created our first organization. This is the start of a long journey into Azure DevOps. In addition to creating the organization, we learned about some of the settings available at the organization level. So, in the next chapter, let us move on to create a project within the created organization.

Chapter 2
Creating Your First Project

☑ Create new project

☑ Work item process

☑ Basic, Agile, Scrum, CMMI

☑ Project settings

☑ Add administrators

☑ Repository policies

☑ Service connections

In the previous chapter, we were prompted to create a project during the process of creating a new Azure DevOps account. But in this section, I am going to create a new project from scratch.

Click on the **New project** button on the top right-hand corner to navigate to the new project creation page.

Figure 16: New project button

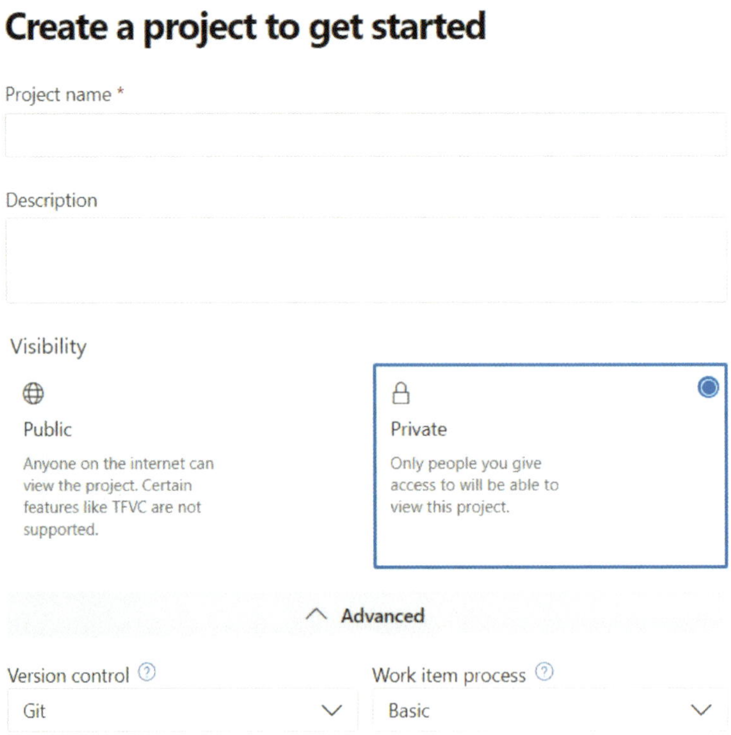

Figure 17: Create project dialog

Provide a suitable name and a description to your project and make it either **Public** or **Private**. Here, you have the possibility to select your version control system for versioning your project resources. By default, it is set to **Git**, which is a distributed version control system. If you prefer a centralized version control system, then you can use the **TFVC** option.

In addition to that, you can select which work item process you prefer to choose. There are 4 main options to choose from.

1. Basic
2. Agile
3. Scrum
4. CMMI

Let us have a brief look into these different work item processes.

Basic

This is the simplest model you can choose out of the four. It has only 3 work item types (WITs)

1. Epic ← Portfolio backlog
2. Issue ← Product backlog
3. Task

These 3 work item types help us to organize our work in a hierarchical way. **Task** is the smallest unit. **Issue** is the parent of **Task**, and **Epic** is the parent of **Issue**. Epic comes under portfolio backlog which lets you to organize your work starting from a high-level business perspective. Following are some examples for **Epics**.

- Improve the user friendliness and user experience
- Convert the paper-based quiz into a web-based application

Issues on the other hand, focus more on implementing the Epics on a feature basis. An issue can be considered as a shippable feature of the product. Following are some examples of Issues.

- Add a login functionality
- Create a notification feature
- Add new icons to improve look and feel
- Design a new colour scheme

Issues can be further divided into small tasks. Usually, these tasks should not take more than one day to complete. So, the whole purpose of each task is to implement/fix a given issue.

Agile

This is good for teams using Agile planning. Here, the development and test activities are tracked separately.

Following are the main WITs associated with Agile process.

1. Epic
2. Feature
3. User Story
4. Bug
5. Task

Epic and **Feature** are on the top level, and **User Story** and **Bug** can be managed separately. You can create Tasks for both User Story and Bug. Like the Basic process, you can group your work items according to your needs. Here, you have more flexibility to organize your work than the Basic process. However, the concepts are basically the same described under the Basic process.

Scrum

If your team is supposed to practice Scrum, then this is the most suitable type for you. It is quite like Agile where **User Story** is replaced by **Product Backlog Item** (PBI), and **Issue** is replaced by **Impediment**.

CMMI (Capability Maturity Model Integration)

This process can be used if your team follows a more formal approach that requires a framework for improving the process and decision making. It is possible to track requirements, change requests, risks and reviews.

Now, we have some understanding about the work item process. So, in this project, I am going to select the simplest process - **Basic**. Click on the **Create Project** /**Save** button to create the new project.

Now you have created your first Azure DevOps project for your organization. The project summary page is shown in Figure 18.

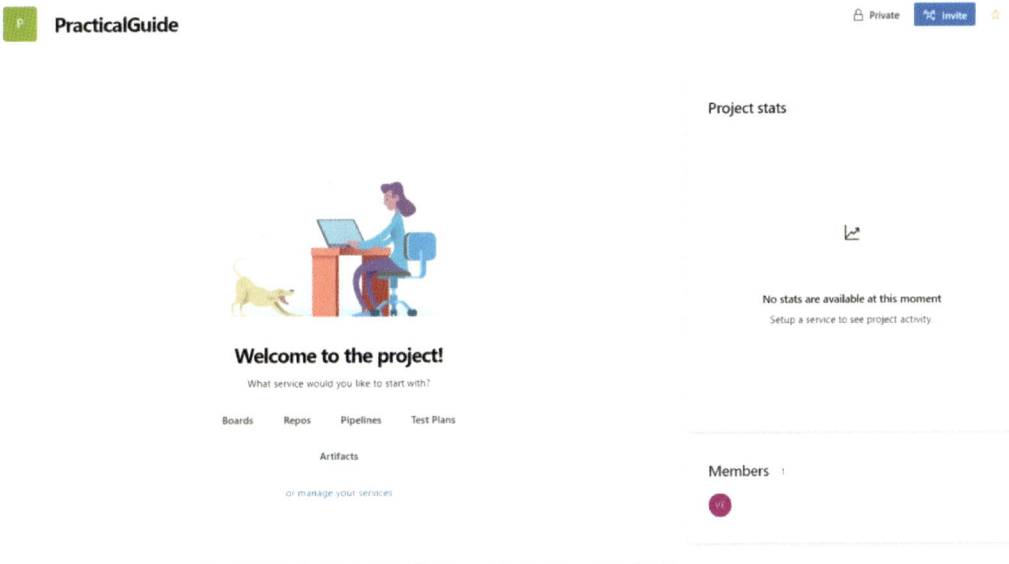

Figure 18: Project summary page

Project Settings

In this section, I will highlight some of the most important settings under the project section. To access the settings page, navigate to your project and click on the **Project Settings** link on the bottom left hand corner.

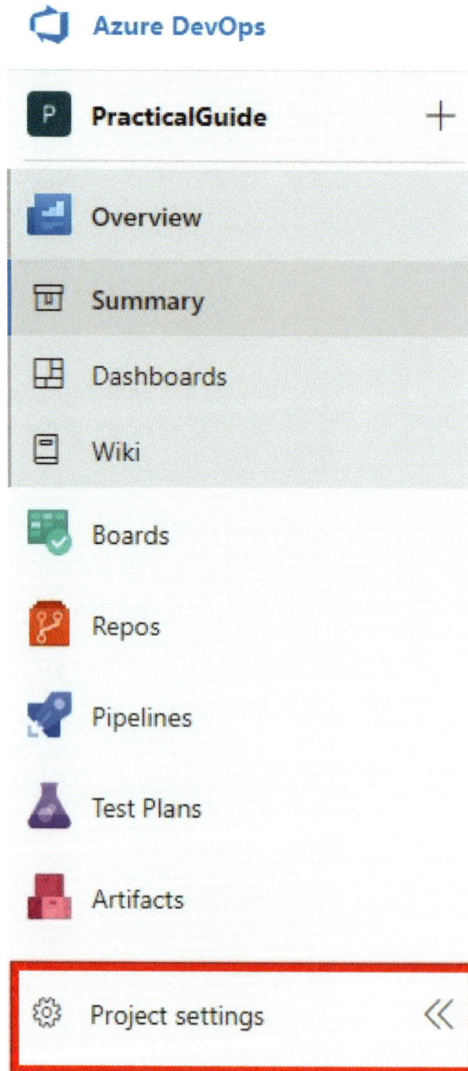

Figure 19: Project settings link

General -> Overview

Here, you can rename your project, change the work item process and visibility of the project etc. However, be careful when changing the work item process, as it can be a breaking change and you have to manually fix states of your tasks.

In addition to that, you can add more administrators to the project by clicking on the **Add administrator** button.

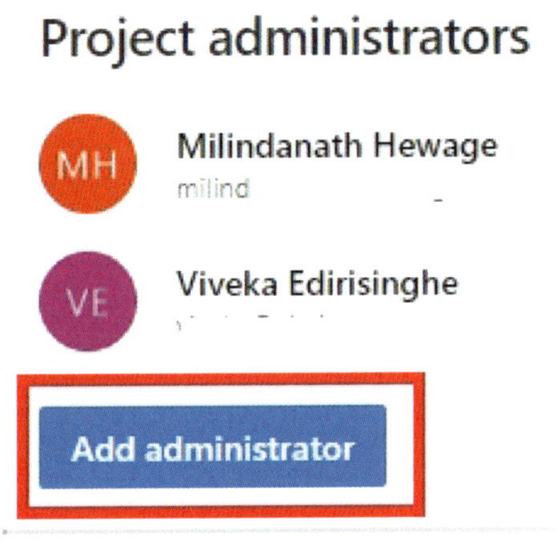

Figure 20: Add administrator

Another nice feature that you can change here is the Azure DevOps services.

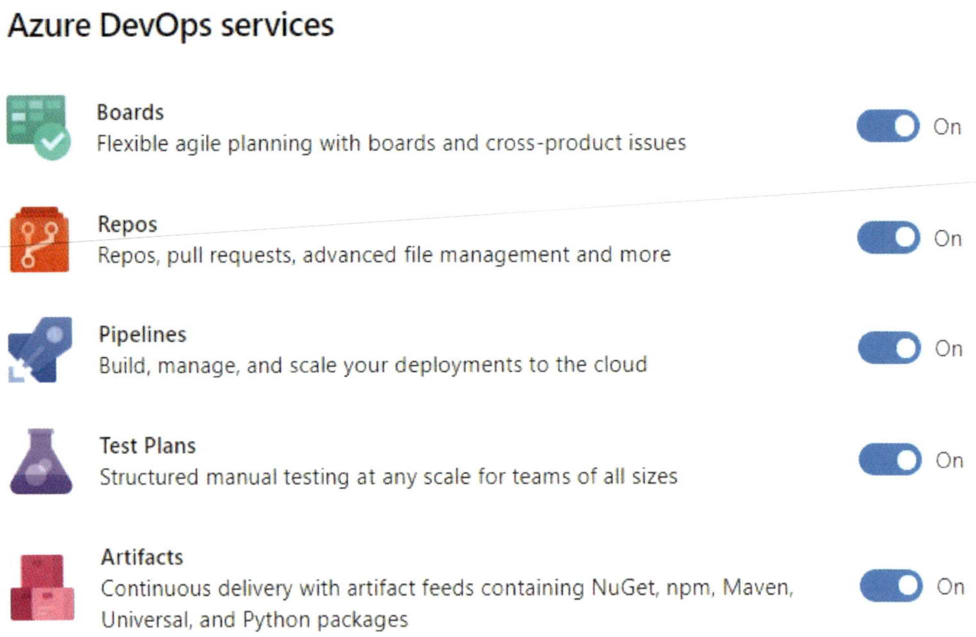

Azure DevOps services

Boards
Flexible agile planning with boards and cross-product issues   On

Repos
Repos, pull requests, advanced file management and more   On

Pipelines
Build, manage, and scale your deployments to the cloud   On

Test Plans
Structured manual testing at any scale for teams of all sizes   On

Artifacts
Continuous delivery with artifact feeds containing NuGet, npm, Maven, Universal, and Python packages   On

Figure 21: Azure DevOps services

Here, you can turn on/off different Azure DevOps services. For example, if you only need a place to store your source code, then you can only turn on *Repos* and turn off all the other features.

General -> Teams

You might have several teams working on the same project. For example, a developer team, sales team or a support team. That can be done under this section. In addition to that, you can add users to different teams.

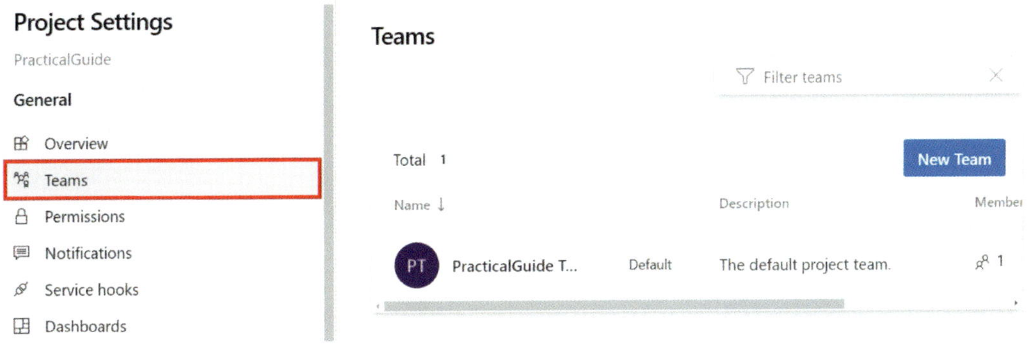

Figure 22: General -> Teams settings

General -> Permissions

This section is more or less the same as the permission in the organization settings. But in this case, these permissions you set here will only be applicable to the current project.

General -> Service hooks

Here, you can integrate with third party software/applications. For example, say your support team uses Zendesk as their software to register tickets considering customer issues, then you can integrate those tickets with Azure DevOps using a service hook.

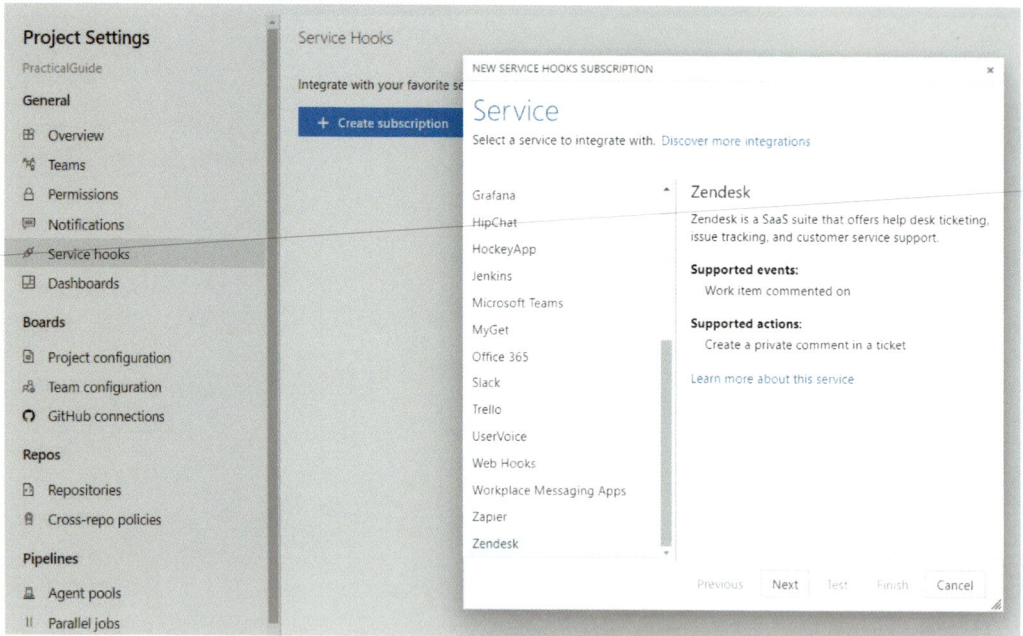

Figure 23: Service hooks

Boards -> Team configuration

Here you can set which working days, the team is working on this project.

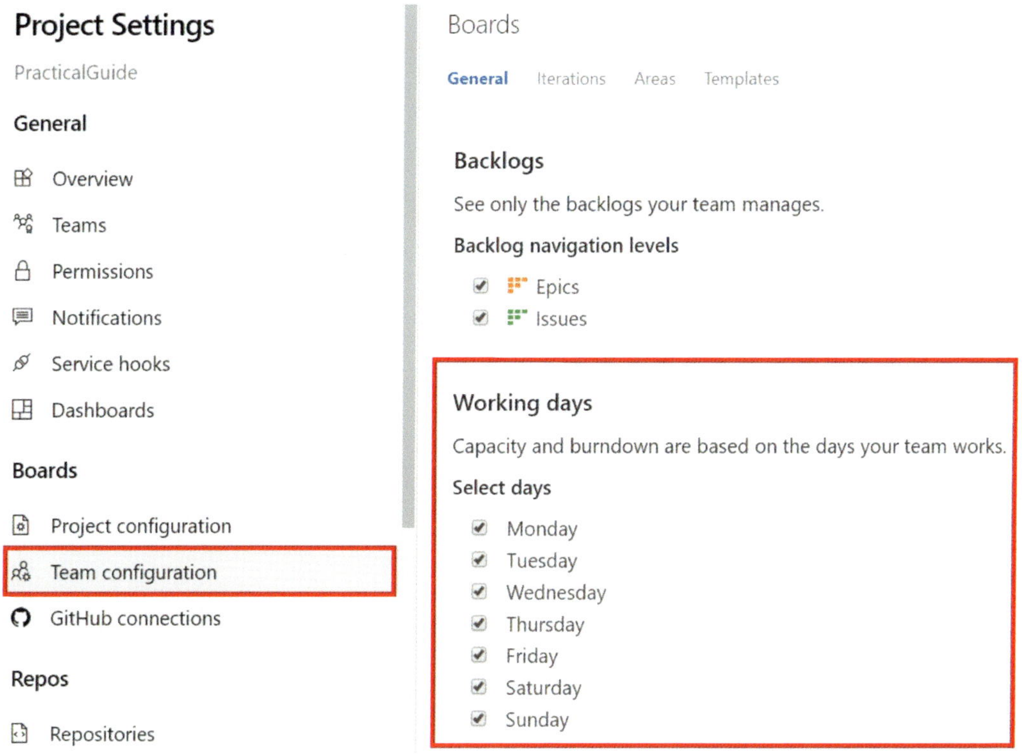

Project Settings

PracticalGuide

General

⊞ Overview

⁂ Teams

🔓 Permissions

▤ Notifications

✎ Service hooks

⊞ Dashboards

Boards

▣ Project configuration

⅍ Team configuration

○ GitHub connections

Repos

▣ Repositories

Boards

General   Iterations   Areas   Templates

Backlogs

See only the backlogs your team manages.

Backlog navigation levels

☑ ⣿ Epics

☑ ⣿ Issues

Working days

Capacity and burndown are based on the days your team works.

Select days

☑ Monday

☑ Tuesday

☑ Wednesday

☑ Thursday

☑ Friday

☑ Saturday

☑ Sunday

Figure 24: Working days under Team configuration

Boards -> GitHub connections

To connect your GitHub account, click on the button **Connect your GitHub account**. After you have given authorization to GitHub to access the project, then you can select which GitHub project you want to associate with this project.

Figure 25: Connect GitHub with Azure Boards

Repos -> Repositories

Here you can either create a new repository or edit security, options and policies of an existing repository.

Repos -> Cross-repo policies

If you want to protect certain branches of your source code, then you can use this settings page. Click on the **Add branch protection** button to load the modal dialog to add branch protection. For example, if you want to protect the default branch (usually the master branch), you select the first option. If your release branches are located in the **releases** folder, then you can use the second option to protect all your release branches as shown in Figure 26.

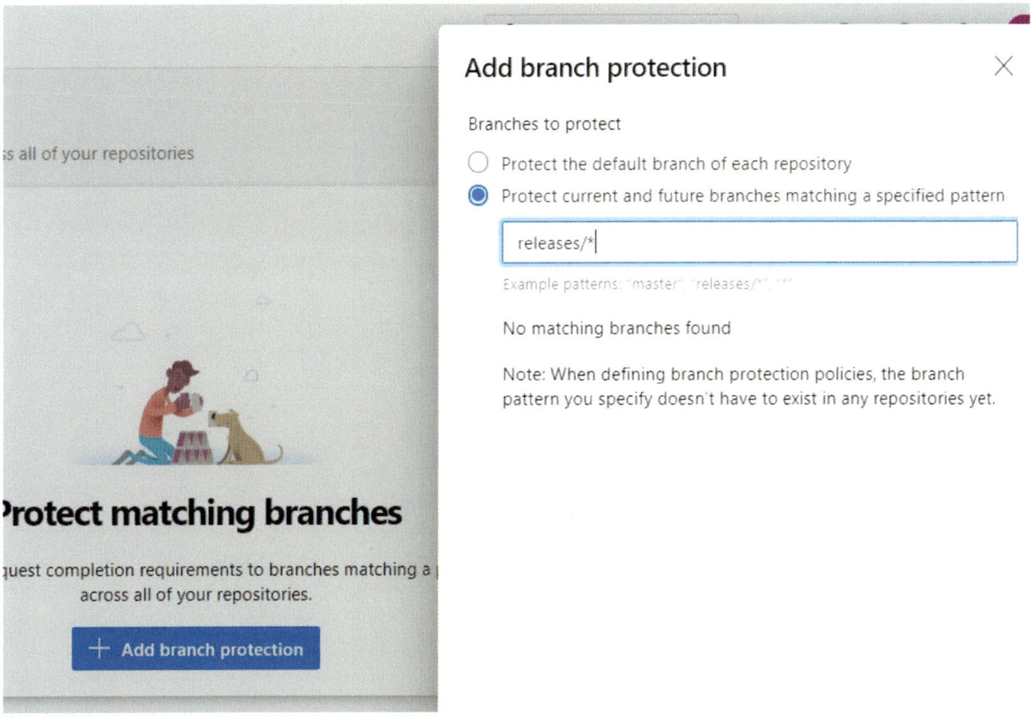

Figure 26: Add branch protection

After you have done that, you get more options to protect your branches. For example, you can add a minimum number of reviewers to approve a certain pull request to that branch. In addition to that, you might always want every commit to the branch be linked to an associated work item. Likewise, you can apply many policies according to your need.

Summary

In this chapter, we investigated creating a new project and some of the settings that we can use to control the project structure and behaviour. Although there are so many things to discuss in these settings, the focus of this book is to minimize details and do some practical tasks with the tool. However, we will come back to some of these settings when we work on Azure Boards, Repos and Pipelines.

Chapter 3
Azure Boards

What you will learn in this chapter

☑ Azure Boards

☑ Tracking work

☑ Work item process (WIP)

☑ Basic, Agile, Scrum

☑ Manage work items

☑ Backlogs

☑ Sprint planning

☑ Queries

☑ Widgets

Azure boards is the place, where you can track the work of your team, using work items. In this book, I have used the **Basic** work item process, which is the simplest work item process in Azure DevOps which contains only 3 work item types (WITs).

1. Epic
2. Issue
3. Task

To access Azure Boards, navigate to your project and click on **Boards** menu item on the left.

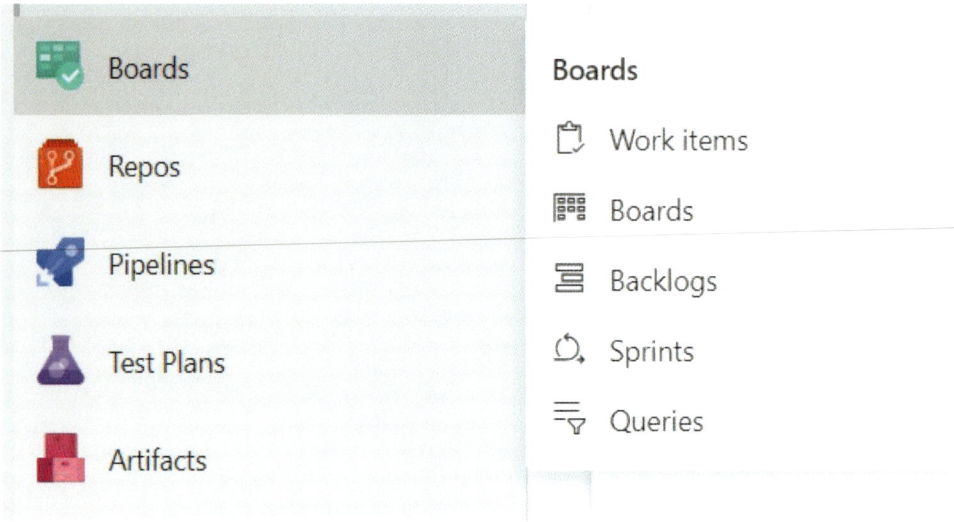

Figure 27: Azure Boards menu

There are 5 sub menu items under Boards.

1. Work items
2. Boards
3. Backlogs
4. Sprints
5. Queries

Work items

Use this, when you want to create a new work item of any type or see all the work items you and your team members have created. To create a new work item, click on **New Work Item** button.

Throughout this book, we use a simple application called MyQuiz to demonstrate real world use of Azure DevOps. However, before starting with the source code, it is quite important that we plan the work and create a backlog of tasks. As mentioned above, click on the **New Work**

Item button to create your first work item. Then select **Issue** as the work item type.

In **Basic** Work Item Process, there is a hierarchy between work item types. Epic is the top level and Task is the lowest. You can decide if you use the Epic level or Issue level as the top work item type for your project.

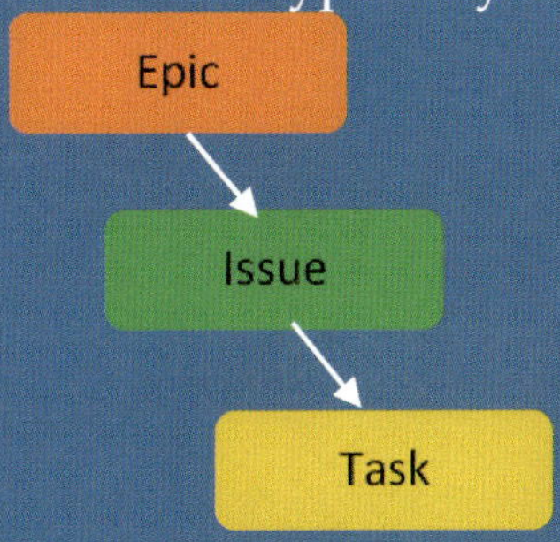

Epic

Issue

Task

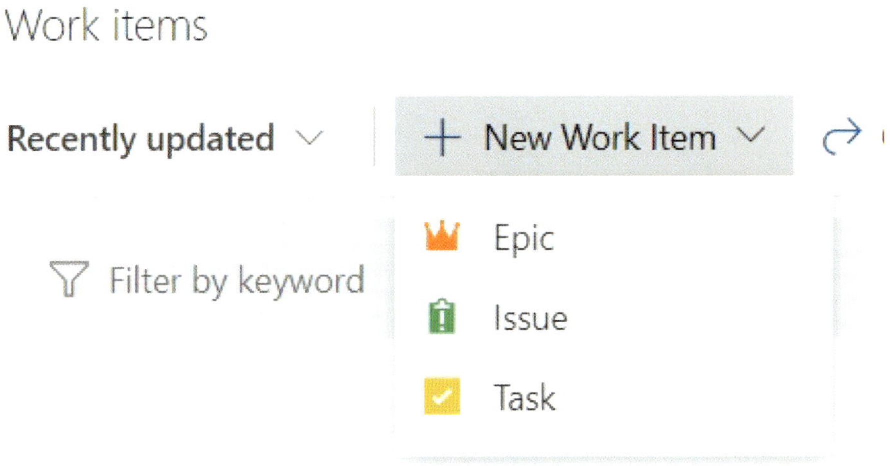

Work items

Recently updated ∨ | + New Work Item ∨ ⤳ ⁞

▽ Filter by keyword

👑 Epic

🔋 Issue

✅ Task

Figure 28: Creating a new work item

New Work Item dialog box for an **Issue** is shown in Figure 29. Let us try to understand some of the important information that we need to fill in, when creating a new work item.

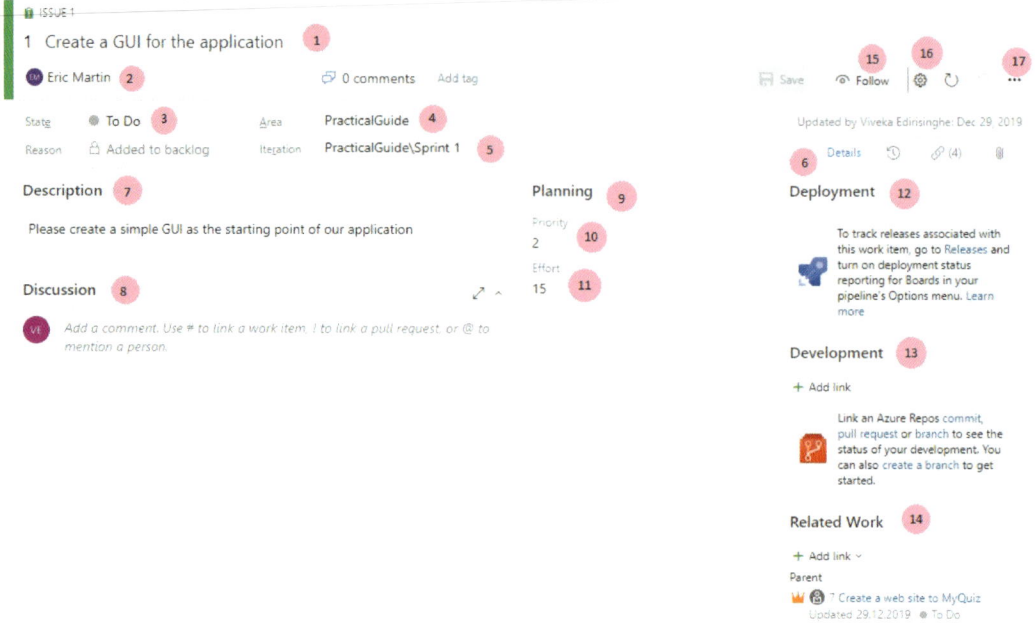

Figure 29: Create new issue window

It is mandatory to provide a title for the new issue **1** . Then, you can assign it to a particular member of your team **2** . Leave it as "**unassigned**" if you have not decided who is going to work on the issue. By default, the initial state of every issue is set to "**To Do**" **3** . Basic work item process provides you 3 states, *To Do – Doing – Done*. You can later change into a different state when you are working on the issue. In addition to that, you can assign this to an **Area** **4** and specify in which iteration this task is going to be fixed **5** . As we have not planned any iterations yet, we can keep the default value for now.

Create new work item page is divided into 4 sections **6** .

Details tab

The **details** tab is selected by default. Inside that, there is the **Description** area [7] , where you can describe the issue in detail. If you need to collaborate with other members of the team and want to make any comments related to the issue, then you can use the **Discussion** section. [8]

Under the **Planning** section [9] you can specify the **Priority** [10] (1 is the highest priority) of the task and the **Effort** [11] you need to put to complete the issue. You can select a unit best suits you, for example it could be in hours or days. Setting a value to **effort** is important when we break our work into small iterations.

If you select a work item of type **Task**, you will get the option to specify the *Remaining Work* instead of *Effort*.

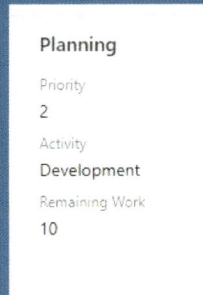

Planning

Priority
2

Activity
Development

Remaining Work
10

Deployment section [12] will show all the releases that are associated with this work item. Under **Development** [13] , you can either link a commit done to the source code, a branch of the source code or a pull request, or it will be automatically linked when there is a development link related to this work item. Under **Related Work** [14] , it shows the other work items that have any relationship to this issue.

History tab

Under **history** tab, you can see all the changes done to this issue throughout its life cycle, via graphically and textually.

Links tab

Here, you have the possibility to link an existing work item, a commit to the source code, branch, a pull request etc. In other words, all the links connected to **Development** [13] and **Related Work** [14] will be shown under this section.

Attachments tab

The last tab is the **attachments** tab, where you can attach any images, documents etc. related to the issue.

On the top right-hand corner of the window, you will find some other actions regarding the issue. For example, you can follow this issue [15] and get notifications when a certain event occurs related to the issue. Notification settings can be modified by clicking on the gear icon [16] next to follow button. In addition to that, there is a context menu [17] where you can perform additional work related to the issue. These options are shown in Figure 30. After you have filled all the necessary information, you can click on the **Save & Close** button to save the changes you made.

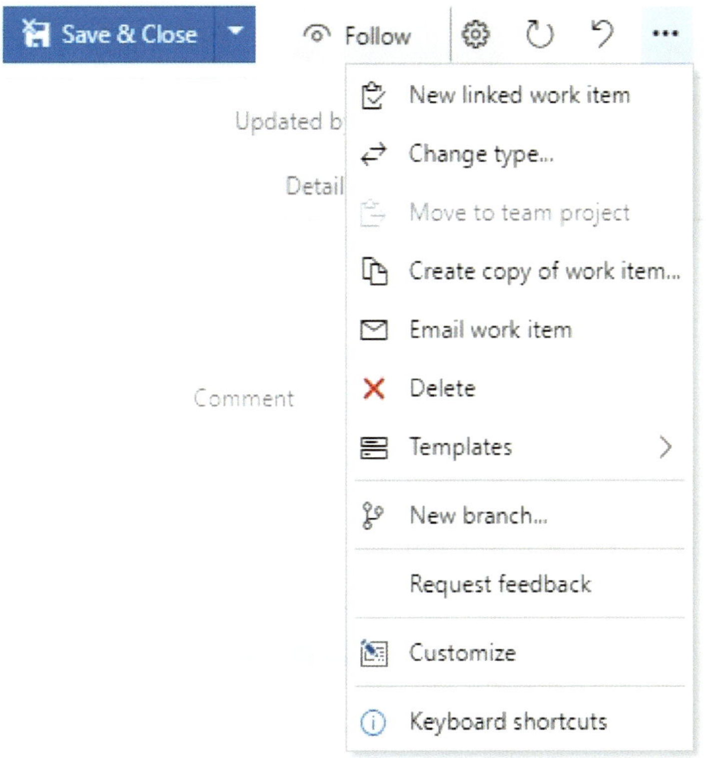

Figure 30: Context menu for additional functionality

Once you have created an **Issue**, it will be shown in the Work items list.

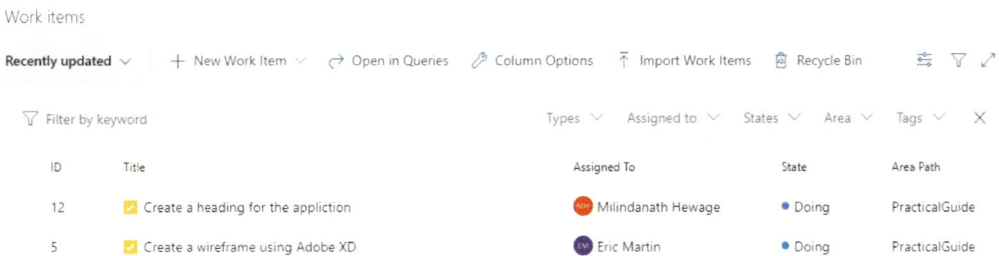

Figure 31: Created issues shown in a list

You can change the work item type by clicking on the ellipsis icon next to the title and then clicking on the **Change type** menu item.

> Each work item has a unique number as its identifier. This number increments sequentially for every work item you create in your organization. Keep in mind that it does not start from 1 for each project as it is organization based.

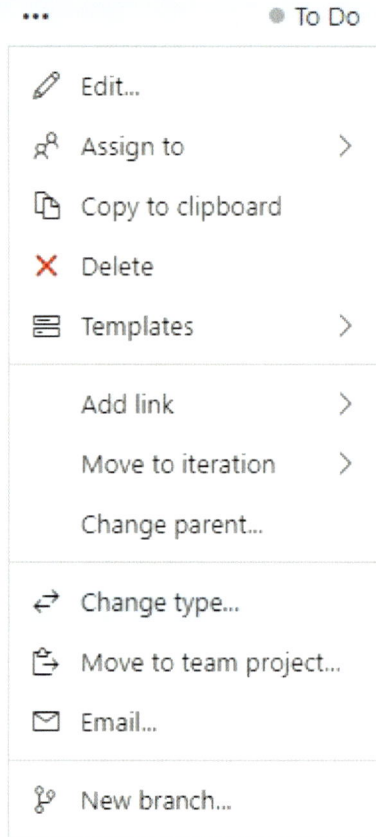

	● To Do

```
✏  Edit...
ⱥ  Assign to              >
⎘  Copy to clipboard
✕  Delete
☰  Templates              >
   ─────────────────────
   Add link               >
   Move to iteration      >
   Change parent...
   ─────────────────────
⇄  Change type...
↱  Move to team project...
☐  Email...
   ─────────────────────
ያ  New branch...
```

Figure 32: Change work item type

Then select the new work item type you want to change from the **Type** dropdown menu. You can also add a **reason** why you change the type. Click the **OK** button to complete the change process.

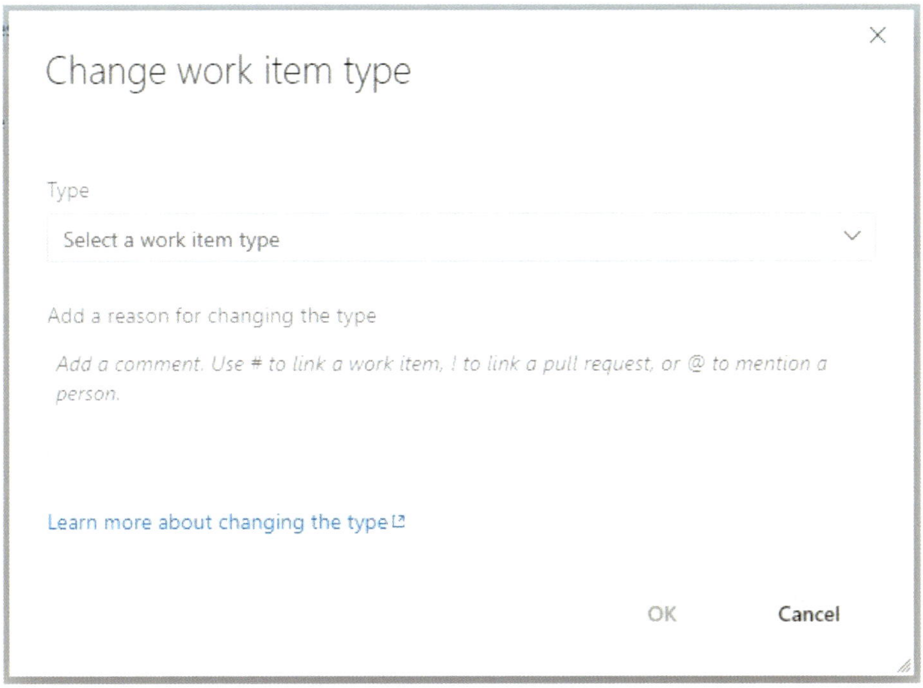

Figure 33: Change work item type dialog

Boards

After you have created all the work items for the project, then you can view those items in two different ways.

1. As a Kanban board or
2. As a backlog

By navigating to the Boards section, you can see a board view of your tasks as shown in Figure 34.

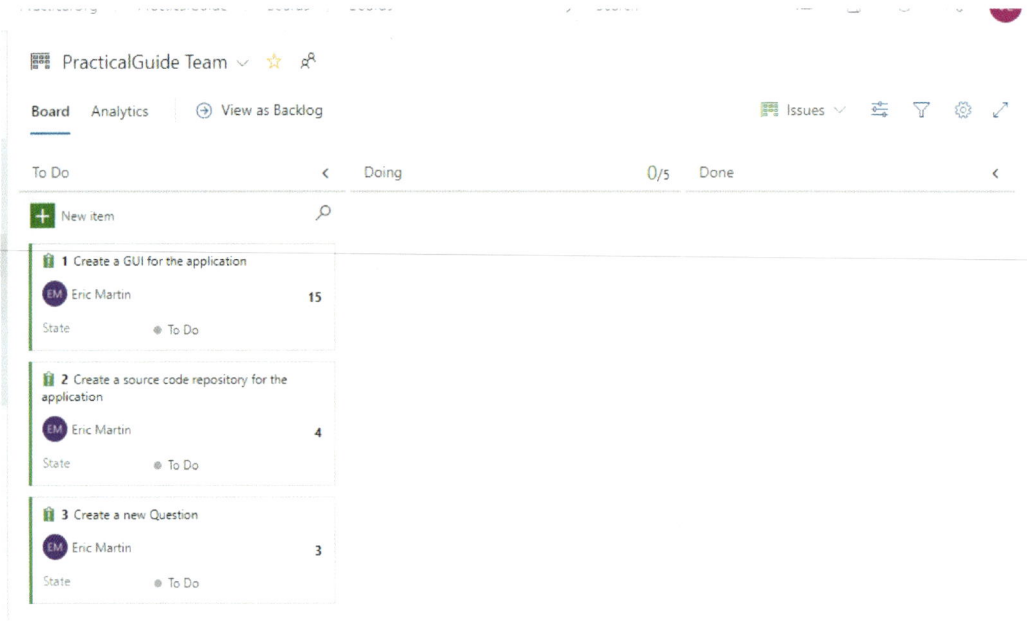

Figure 34: Kanban Board view of the backlog

The board has 3 columns to match the 3 states provided by the **Basic** Work item process. Those are **To Do, Doing** and **Done**. The board can be filtered by either Issues or Epics. In Figure 34, it is showing only the Issues. It is possible to create an Issue or an Epic using this board by clicking on the **New item** button in the **To Do** column. Here, you type only the title and the rest you can edit by navigating to the issue itself.

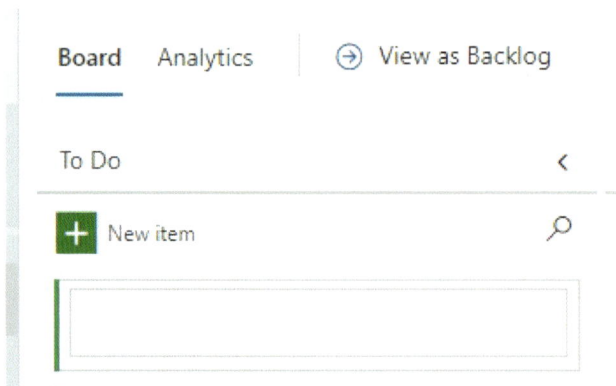

Figure 35: Creating a new item

Each Card on the board is associated with a context menu, where you can do things, such as creating a task or a test case, edit title and so on.

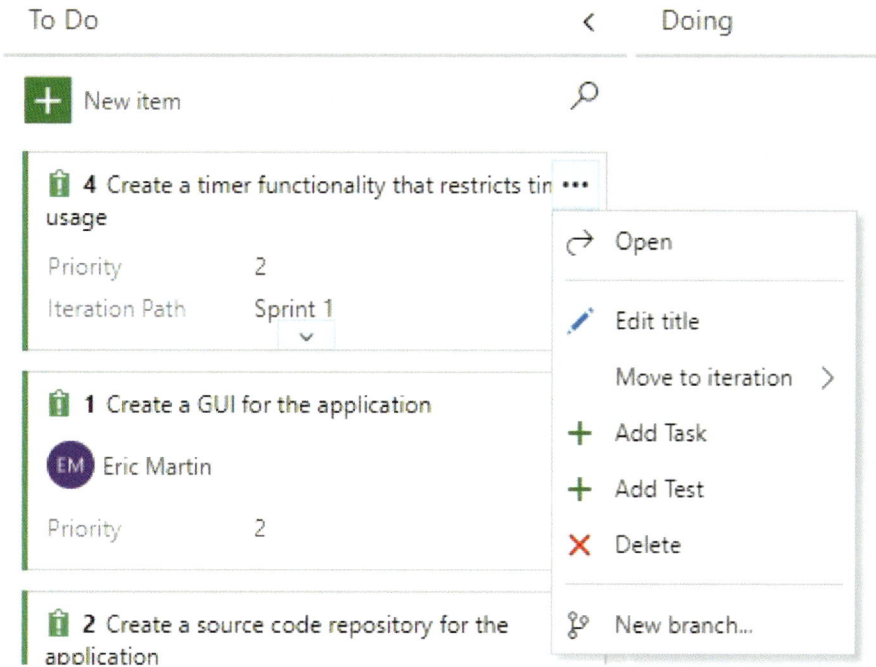

Figure 36: Context menu for additional actions

If you select the **Add Task** item for example, then it will be shown inside the card as shown in Figure 37.

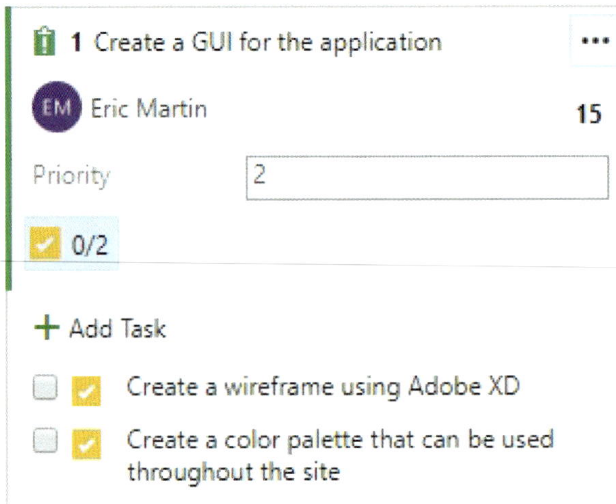

Figure 37: Card of an issue listing all its sub tasks

You can customize the **Board view** according to your needs, as it is configurable. Click on the gear icon on the top right-hand corner to do this. You can customize your cards, Board and General settings on the Kanban board.

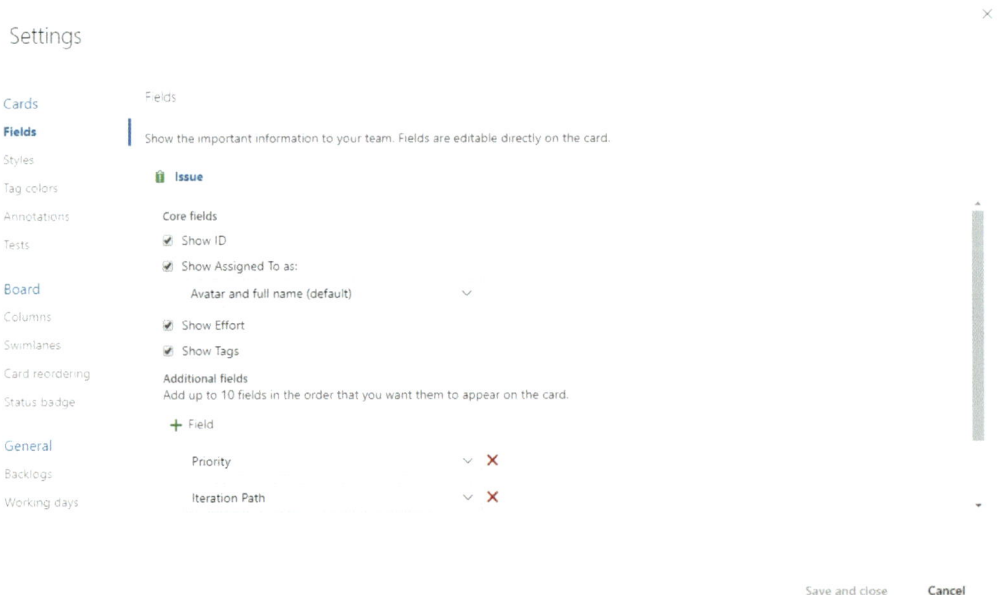

Figure 38: Kanban board settings page

Backlogs

Backlogs is also another way of showing your work items. This view is showing the work items in a list. Similarly, to Boards, you can filter items by Issues or Epics. This backlog view has a side pane on the right-hand side which can be used to plan your work items in different sprints and map your issues to Epics. This can be turned off according to your wish. You can switch between these two modes by clicking on either **Mapping** or **Planning** as shown in Figure 39.

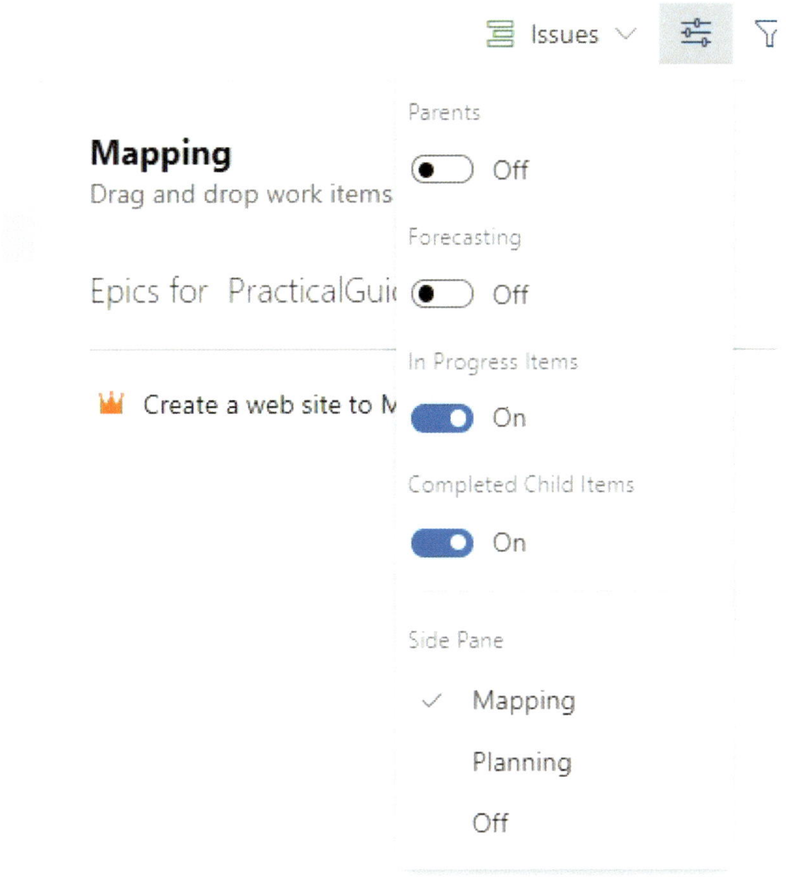

Figure 39: Backlog settings with Mapping and Planning options

Figure 40 shows the mapping side pane where you can drag and drop your issues to an existing Epic.

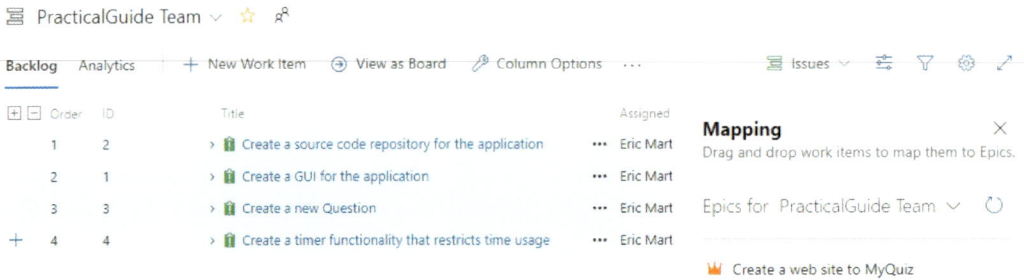

Figure 40: Mapping issues to Epic

> You can select multiple work items by clicking on one issue on the list and holding the Shift key while clicking on the last item you want to select. Use Ctrl key to select multiple items from several random rows. This way you can drag multiple items to the Epic you want to group the issues into.

Sprints

A sprint is a short iteration of your product life cycle. The definition of a sprint given by the Scrum guide is as follows.

The heart of Scrum is a Sprint, a time-box of one month or less during which a "Done", useable, and potentially releasable product Increment is created. Sprints have consistent durations throughout a development effort. A new Sprint starts immediately after the conclusion of the previous Sprint. [2]

So, the final goal of a sprint is to produce a releasable product increment. Keeping that in mind, we have to plan our sprint. Usually, the duration of a sprint is equal to or less than one month. Let us say, our plan is to have 2 weeks lengthy sprints.

> In a sprint, you work on small tasks that usually take less than a day to complete. So, remember to add at least one Task to your issues in the backlog.

First, navigate to **Sprints** sub menu under Azure Boards. The **Basic** process has already created a sprint for us with the name **Sprint 1**. But it is not yet configured properly. So, as the first thing, you need to define the start and the end dates of the sprint. So, click on the **Set dates** link on the top right-hand corner.

No iteration dates
Set dates

Sprint 1 ∨   Person: All ∨

Figure 41: Set dates for the sprint

Specify the dates as shown in Figure 42.

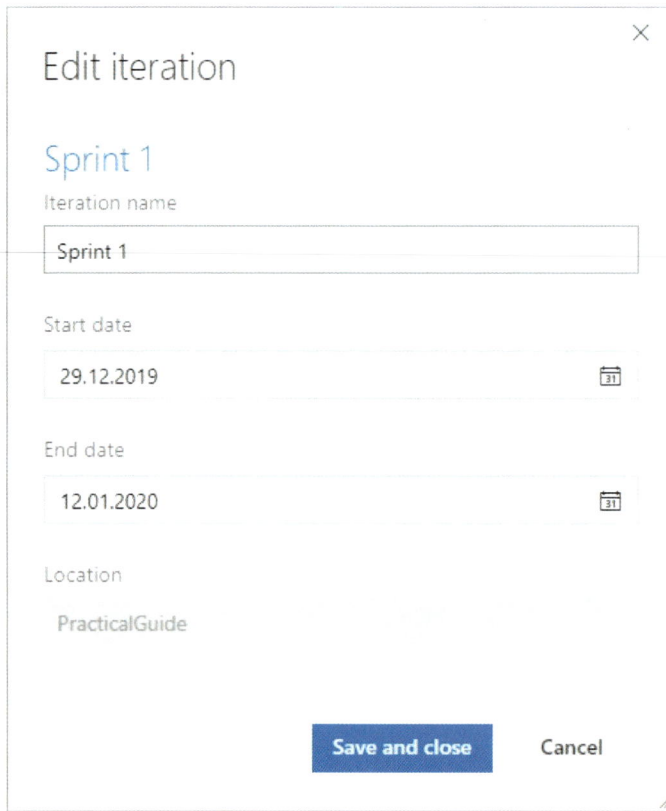

Figure 42: Edit iteration page

Planning the sprint

Planning the 2 weeks of the sprint is quite important to reach your goal at the end of the sprint. First, go to the **Sprints** sub menu item and click on the gear icon to set the working days of your sprint. As shown in Figure 43, we have planned to work only on weekdays.

Settings

General

Backlogs

Working days

Working days

Capacity and burndown are based on the days your team works.

Select days

- ☑ Monday
- ☑ Tuesday
- ☑ Wednesday
- ☑ Thursday
- ☑ Friday
- ☐ Saturday
- ☐ Sunday

Figure 43: Working days settings

Suppose we have 2 developers working on the project and each of them is working 6 hours a day. Click on the **Capacity** link to plan your sprint.

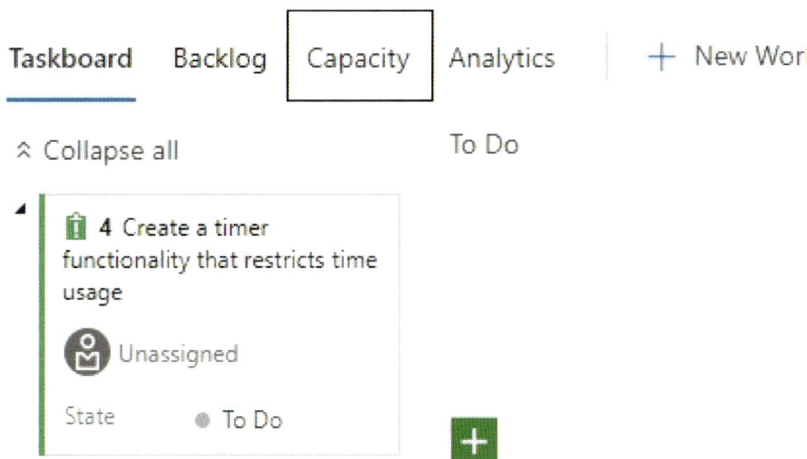

Taskboard   Backlog | Capacity | Analytics | + New Wor

≫ Collapse all   To Do

> 📋 4 Create a timer
> functionality that restricts time
> usage
>
> 👤 Unassigned
>
> State   ● To Do

+

Figure 44: Capacity planning link

As shown in Figure 45, the two developers working 6 hours a day and they are both doing development. If one person is involved in several activities like *Design, Requirements, Deployment* etc., then you can add them here as well.

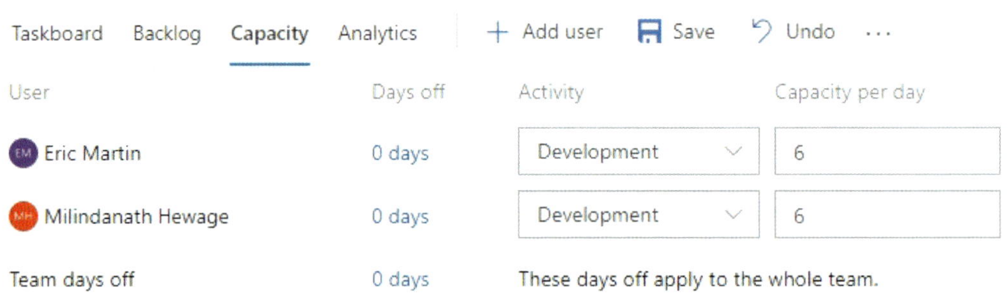

Figure 45: Capacity planning for two members

Before the start of the sprint, *Eric Martin* says he is planning to have 2 days off during the sprint. So, we have to take that into account and plan for that. Click on **0 days** link in front of *Eric Martin* to add that information.

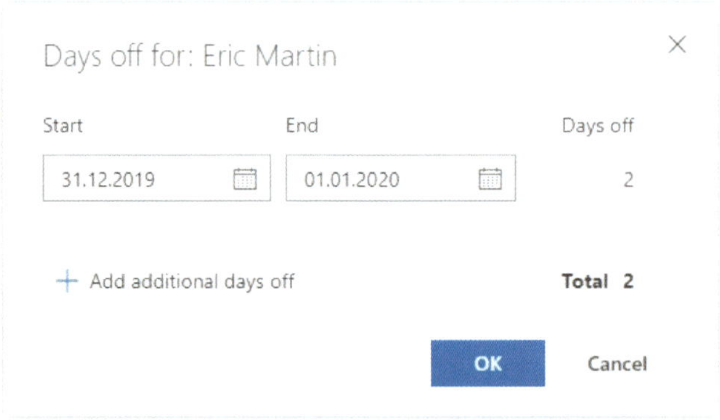

Figure 46: Day offs for individual team members

During the sprint planning meeting, both found that they have to participate in another meeting not related to this project during the course of the sprint. So, they need to exclude that day from the planning. So, click on the **0 days** link in front of the **Team days off** and set that date as a day off.

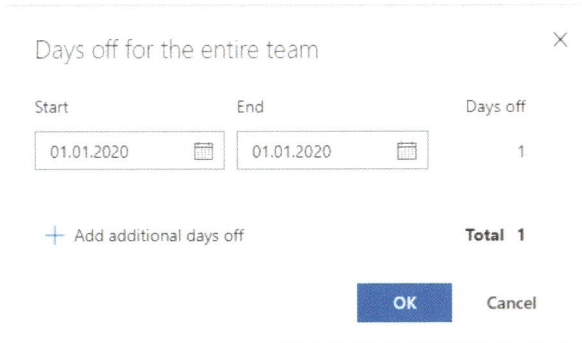

Figure 47: Days off for the entire team

Now the capacity planning is completed and click on the **Save** button to save all your changes. Now click on the **Backlogs** sub menu under Azure DevOps, and on the right-hand side you can see the **Planning / Work Details** panes. Now you can drag and drop which **Issues** you will be fixing in **Sprint 1**.

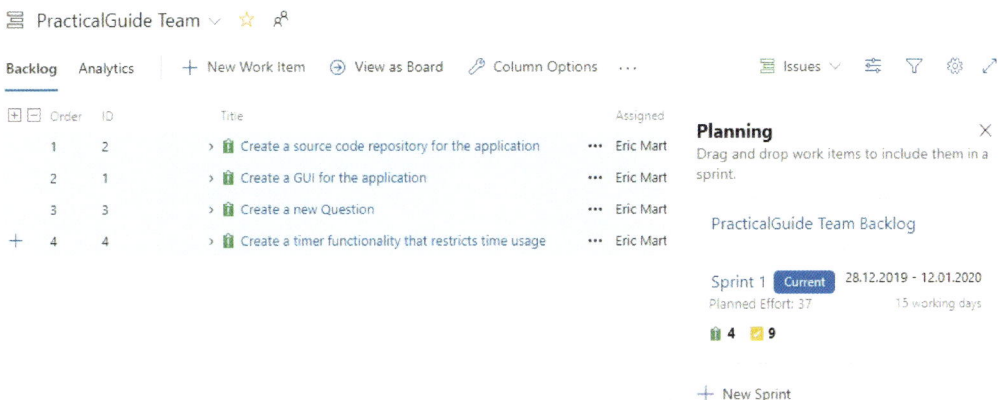

Figure 48: Backlog with planning

After you have assigned all the backlog item issues which will be considered in the current sprint, go back to the **Sprints** sub menu. If you know who is going to work on which task, then it is better to use the **Work Details** view to directly assign tasks to the developers. You can drag and drop Tasks to the team member who is supposed to fix that task, as shown in Figure 49.

> Before assigning tasks to the team members, make sure you have filled the **effort** values for Issues, and the **Remaining Work** for the Tasks.

In this example, the whole team has 102 hours to work during the sprint. Erik Martin has 48 hours and Milindanath Hewage has 52 hours. So, it is the responsibility of the team leader to distribute tasks according to the capacity. Make sure not to overestimate or underestimate the work. Try to balance when estimating work.

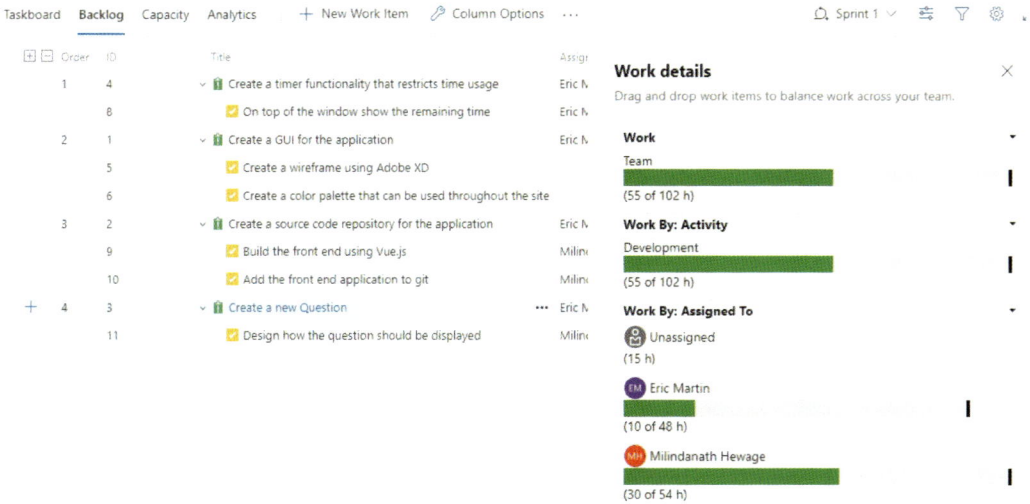

Figure 49: Sprint backlog for Sprint 1 with work details pane

During the sprint

Based on the priority of the tasks, team members can select which tasks they are going to focus on first. Naturally, it is those with the highest priority should be fixed at first. Unfortunately, in Azure DevOps, the backlog board is not automatically sorted by **Priority**. So, you have to arrange your board by dragging and dropping backlog items. Figure 50 shows a backlog board that is ordered manually by its priority.

To Do   ‹

2 Create a source code repository for the application

EM Eric Martin   4

Priority   1
Iteration Path   Sprint 1

✔ 0/2

---

1 Create a GUI for the application

EM Eric Martin   15

Priority   2
Iteration Path   Sprint 1

✔ 0/2

---

3 Create a new Question

EM Eric Martin   3

Priority   3
Iteration Path   Sprint 1

✔ 0/1

---

4 Create a timer functionality that restricts time usage

EM Eric Martin   15

Priority   4
Iteration Path   Sprint 1

✔ 0/1

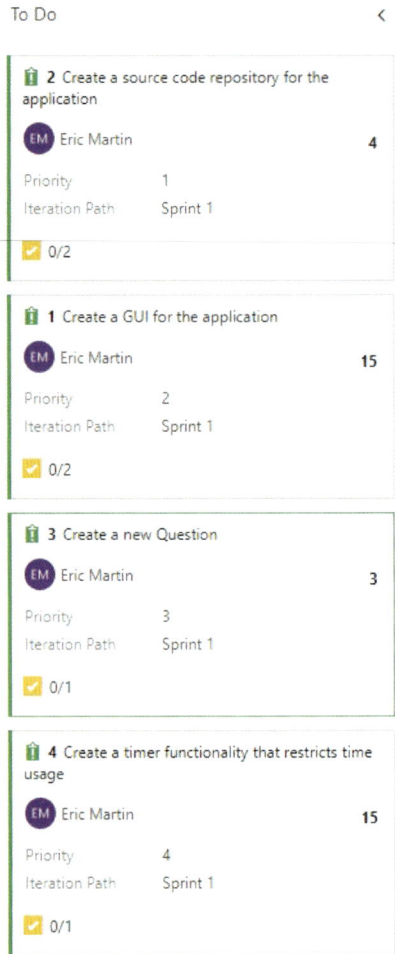

Figure 50: Kanban board sorted by its priority

Once you select a specific item to work on, then drag the task from **To Do** column to **Doing** column to indicate your team, that you are committed to work on that task.

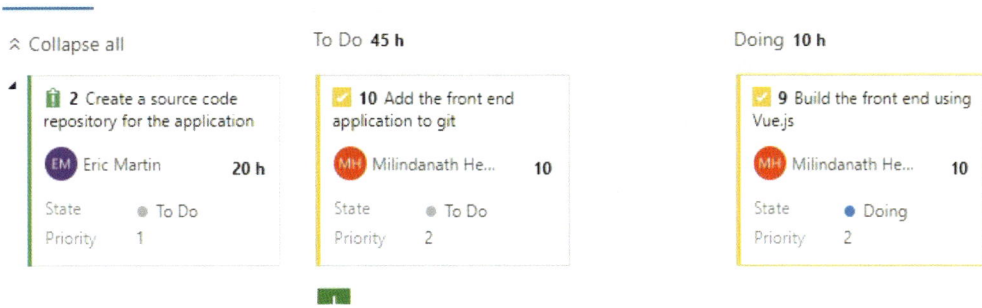

Figure 51: State change from To Do -> Doing

You can move the Task to state **Done** once you have finished your work on that task. When you move a task to the **Done** column, it automatically resets the **Remaining Work** to 0.

Analytics

You can measure the progress of your sprint using the **Analytics** section. Here, you can see the burndown trend of your work items in your Task backlog. You can compare the **ideal trend** and the **actual trend** of your team's work. This might be very helpful to check, how you have planned your work during a sprint and how successful you were doing that. As an example, the burndown chart shown in Figure 52 which shows an overestimated sprint, have failed to achieve the goal at the end of the sprint.

Burndown Trend ⓘ

Start Date	End Date	Backlogs / Work Items	Burndown on	Advanced
12/9/2019 📅 to	12/20/2019 📅	🟨 Tasks backlog ⌄	Sum of Remaining Work ⌄	☐ Show non-working days

12/9/2019 - 12/20/2019

Remaining Work 12
Remaining

Completed 0%   Average 2 burndown   Items not 0 estimated   Total Scope -28.5 Increase

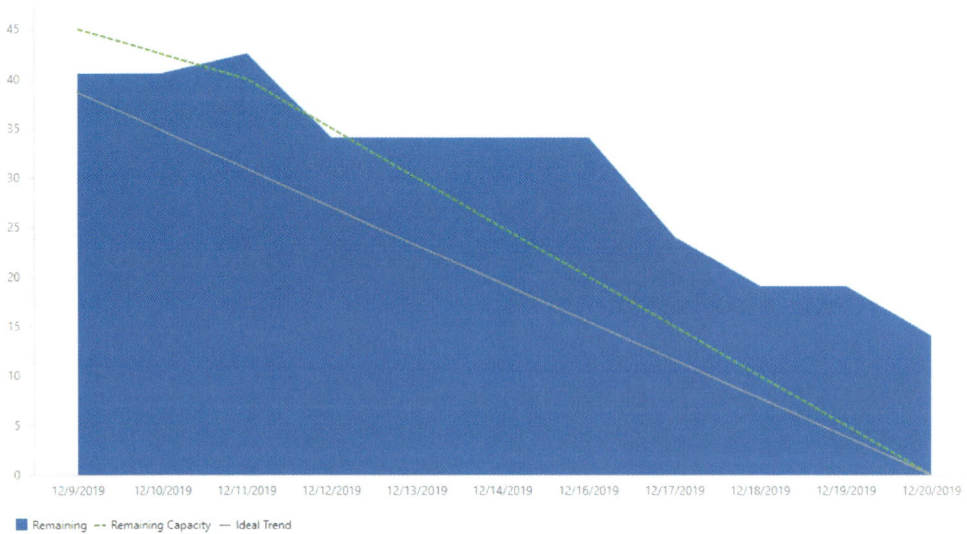

Figure 52: Task burndown trend of a sprint

Queries

Both **Work items** and **Backlog views** we discussed above are predefined. However, if you need to view your own customized backlogs according to your need, then you can use **Queries** for that. Here, you can filter your queries using different field values.

Navigate to the **Queries** sub menu item in Azure Boards. Then you will see the page shown in Figure 53.

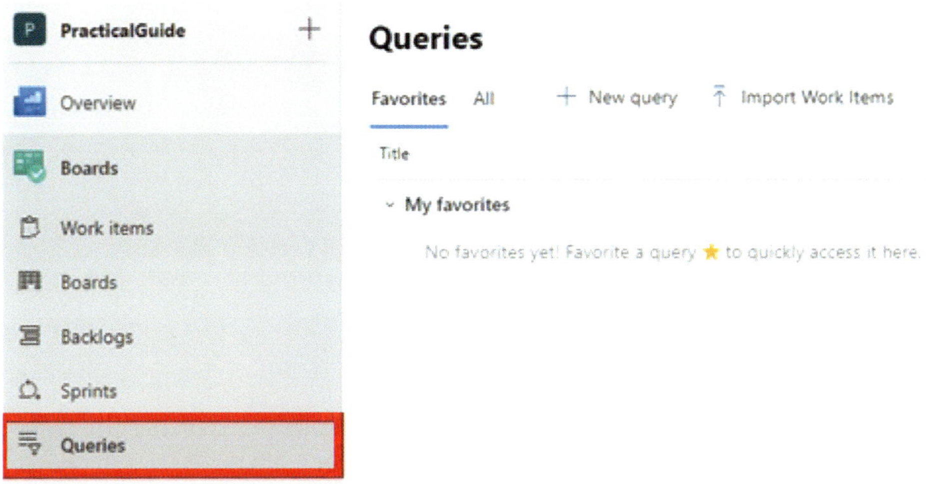

Figure 53: Queries page

You can create a new query by clicking on the **New query** button. Let us create a query to list all the work items which has a **priority** value of **1**. The query should be as follows.

Figure 54: Query for listing Priority 1 work items

Run your query by clicking on the button **Run query**. Now we have one task and one issue with Priority 1. So, the query produces 2 results. Once you are satisfied with the results, you can save the query for later use. So, click on the button **Save query** to save your query. When you save it, you either make it a **shared query** or a **private query** which is only available to you.

ID	Work Item...	Title		Assigned To	State	Tags
2	Issue	Create a source code repository for the application	•••	Eric Martin	To Do	
11	Task	Design how the question should be displayed		Milindanath Hewa...	To Do	

Figure 55: Query results

If you save the query as a shared query, then you have the possibility to show it in the project dashboard. In order to do that, click on **Overview** and then **Dashboards**. Click on **Add a widget** if this is your first time working on the Dashboards section.

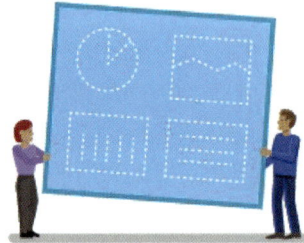

This dashboard doesn't have widgets just yet!

Add one or more widgets to gain visibility into your team's progress.

Add a widget

Figure 56: Add widget

Then search for the value "**Query**" in the add widget search box as shown in Figure 57.

Add Widget

Query

Query Results
Displays results from a query.

Query Tile
Displays the total number of results for a query.

42

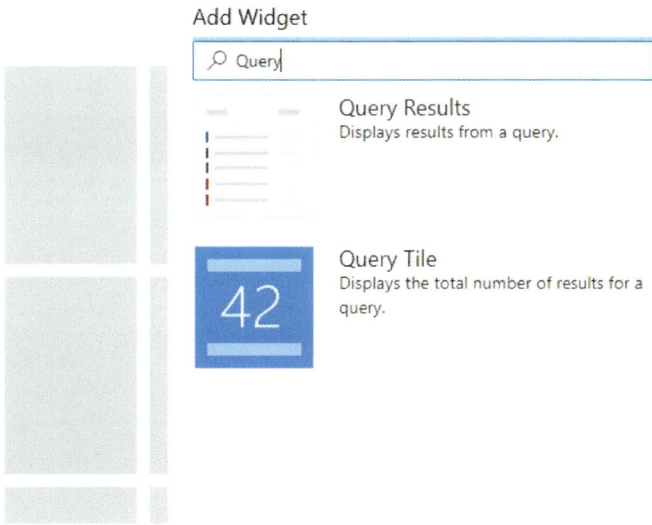

Figure 57: Search for Query Results widget

Then add the **Query Results** widget and click on the gear icon to configure your widget.

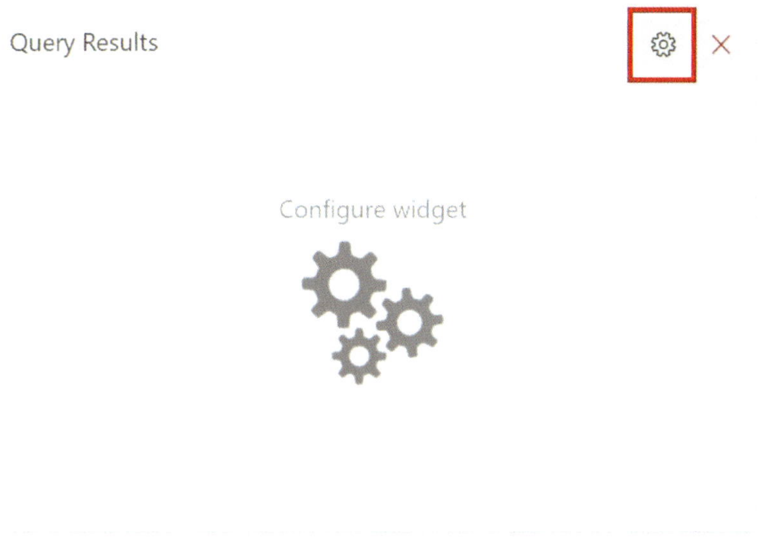

Query Results   ⚙ ✕

Configure widget

Figure 58: Configure widget

Under the settings, provide a suitable name to your widget and select the query you saved under shared queries.

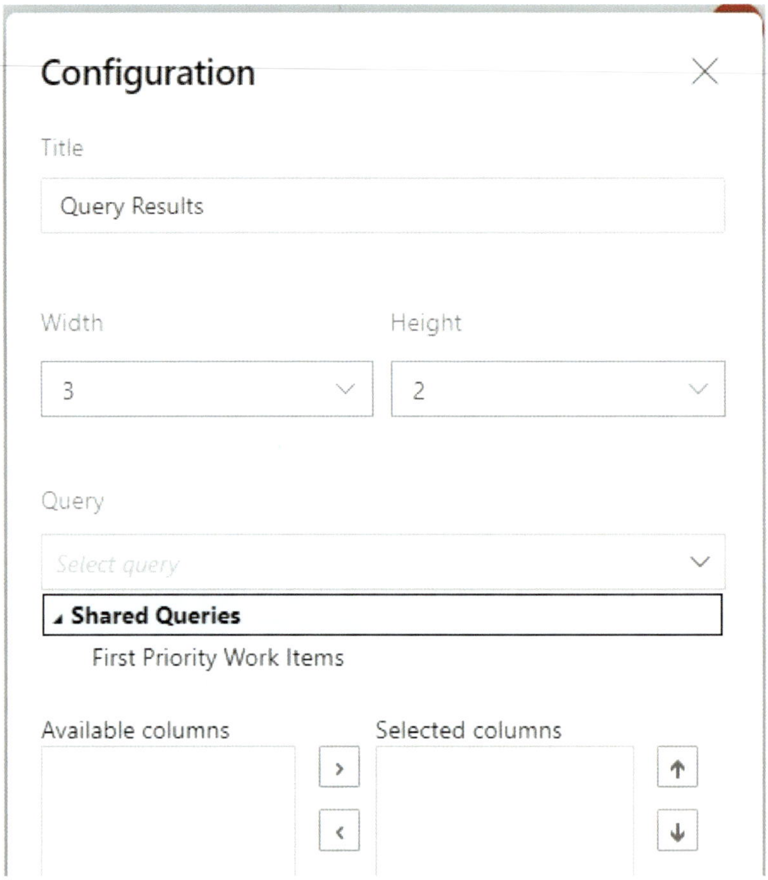

Figure 59: Select and configure the widget

Now you will see the **First Priority Work Items** in the dashboard of your Team project.

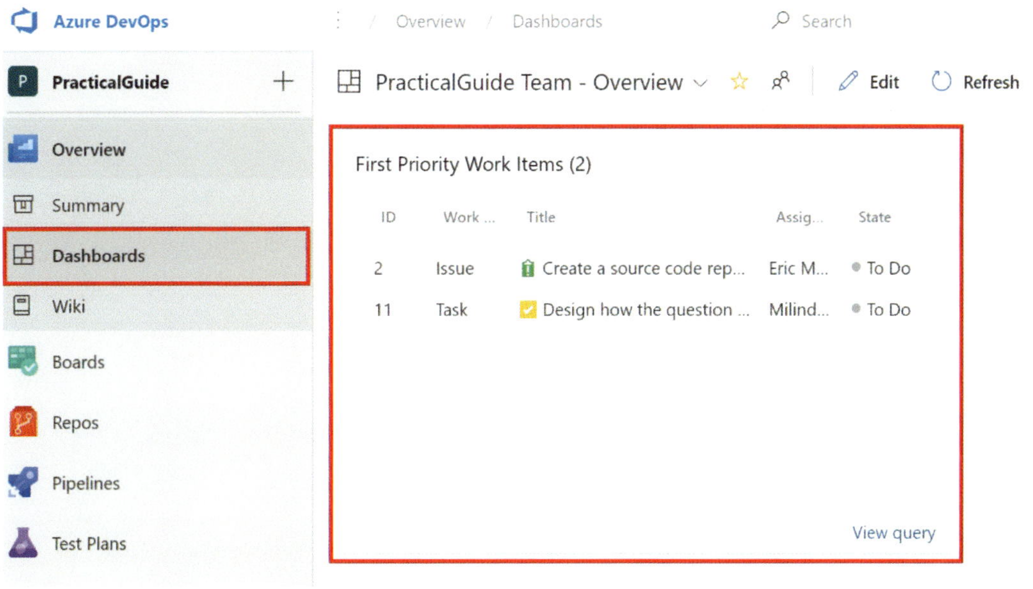

Figure 60: Query results shown in the widget

Summary

In this chapter, we learned the basics of Azure Boards. We used the **Basic** work item process for our project and created our first work item using the Work Items functionality in Azure Boards. Moreover, we went through the Kanban board and backlog views. In addition to that, you learned how to plan a sprint based on the capacity of your team. Finally, you learned how to create customized queries and how to use them in Dashboards of your project.

Chapter 4
Azure Repos

W hen you create a new project in Azure DevOps, you get a new git repository with the same name as your project. You can see this when you click on the side menu item **Repos** as shown in Figure 61. As depicted in the figure, there are several ways you can store your source code and other resources on a remote git repository.

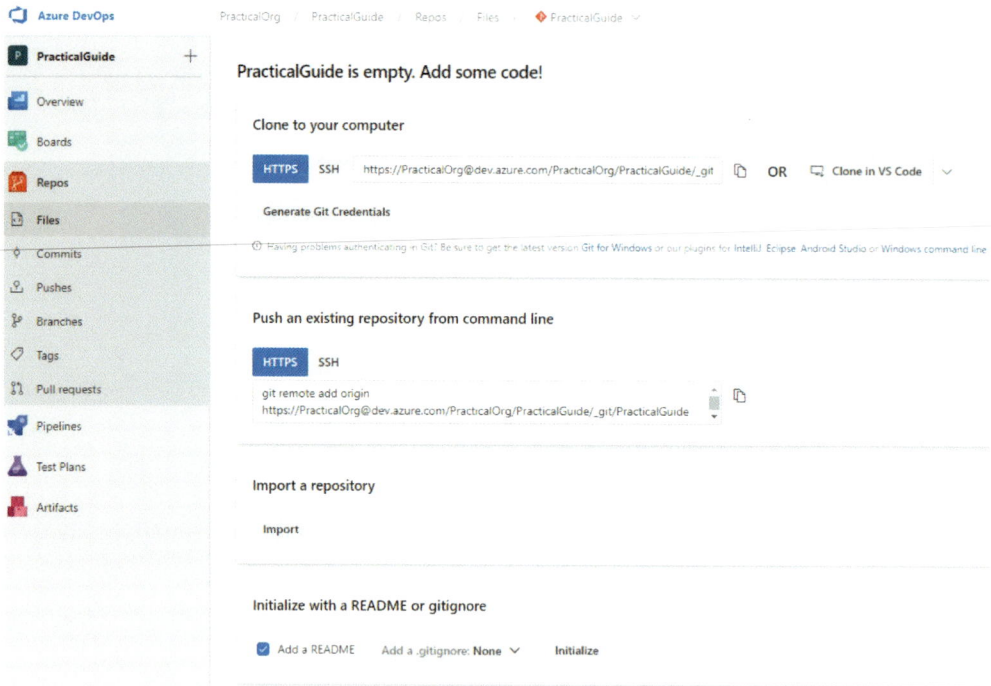

Figure 61: Default Git repository

1. **Clone to your computer. (From Azure Repos to your computer)**
   Using this method, you can take a copy of the repository and download it to a directory in your computer using the following command, or you can directly clone it to Visual Studio Code. However, in this case it will be an empty repository.

   ```
   $ git clone {{your repository URL}}
   ```

2. **Push an existing repository to Azure Repos (From your computer to Azure Repos)**
   You can use this option if you already have your project files inside a folder in your computer. Then it is a matter of just transferring your files from your computer to Azure Repos. The following two commands must be run from your project folder.

   ```
   $ git remote add origin {{your repository URL}}
   ```

```
$ git push -u origin --all
```

3. **Import an existing repository (From another Git Repo to Azure Repos)**
   If you already have a git repository in GitHub, Bitbucket, GitLab or any other location, then you can use this option to import that repository to Azure Repos as shown in Figure 62.

> To issue git commands, you will need to download and install git software to your computer. For windows, download it from https://git-scm.com/download/win

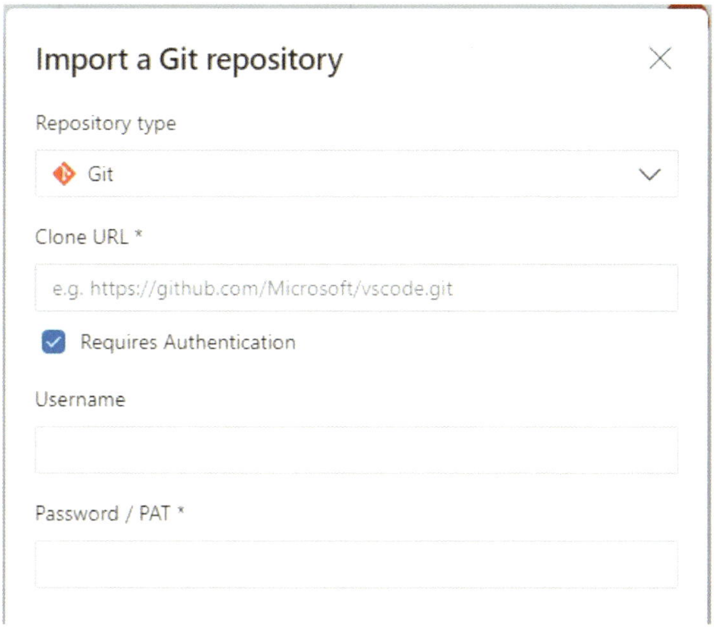

Figure 62: Import an existing repository

MyQuiz – a Vue.js project

Let us create our first application locally and then add it to the source control using the second option shown above. This application is a simple **node.js** application which uses the **Vue.js** framework.

> The focus of this simple application is to demonstrate you the different aspects of Azure Repos and it is not intended to provide you any coding or programming styles or best practices.

Step 1: Install node and npm

If you have not installed node.js on your computer, go ahead and install it from https://nodejs.org/en/. At the time of this writing the version of node is **12.14.0**. This will also install the Node Package Manager (npm) which will be used to download different JavaScript packages for our project.

Step 2: Verify node and npm

Ensure that you have correctly installed node and npm by opening a command prompt and typing the following commands. If you see the version numbers, then your installation is successful.

```
$ node --version
```

```
$ npm --version
```

Step 3: Install vue-cli

Let us use **vue-cli** (Vue Command Line Interface) to create the project. First, create a project folder in your computer. In windows, right click your folder and open Git Bash terminal by clicking on the **Git Bash Here** link.

View		>
Sort by		>
Group by		>
Refresh		
Customise this folder...		
Paste		
Paste shortcut		
Undo Rename	Ctrl+Z	
Open in Visual Studio		
Git GUI Here		
Git Bash Here		
Open with Code		
Share		
View online		
Always keep on this device		
Clear space		
Give access to		>
New		>
Properties		

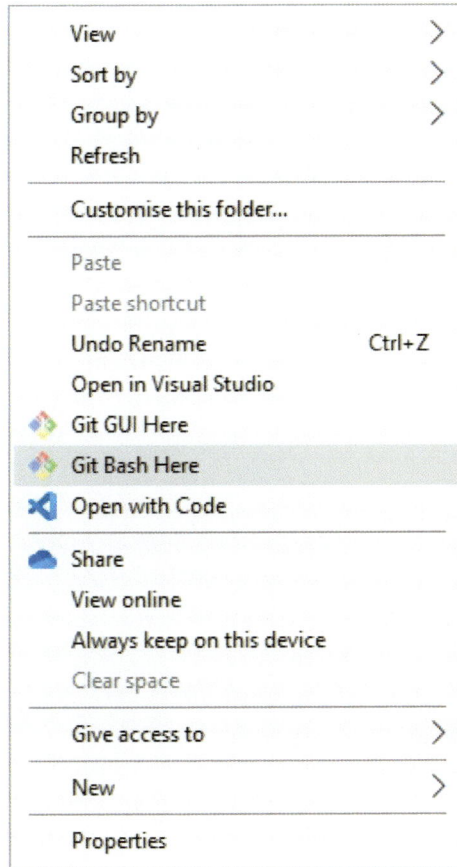

Figure 63: Open Git Bash

Write the following command to install vue-cli globally. The version used here is 4.1.2

```
$ npm install -g @vue/cli
```

Step 4: Install Visual Studio Code

In this book, we use Visual Studio Code as our preferred code editor. But you can choose any other code editor which is suitable for you.

Step 5: Create the project using Vue CLI

Let us try to create the project from Visual Studio Code. So, from your Git Bash terminal, type the following command to open your current folder inside VS Code.

```
$ code .
```

 Click on the menu **view** -> **terminal** to open the built-in terminal in VS Code.

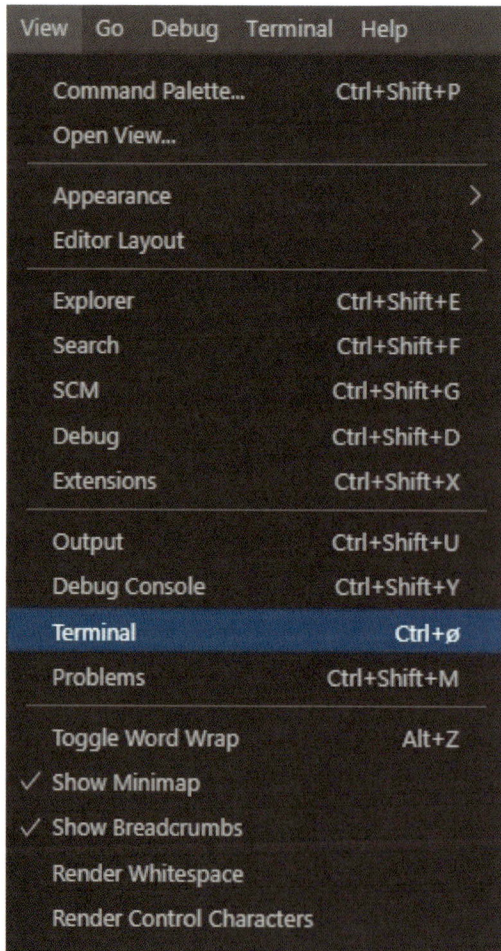

Figure 64: Open terminal in VS Code

Here, you can type the following command to create the project with the name **my-quiz-ui**.

```
$ vue create my-quiz-ui
```

Then, it will ask you to pick a **preset**. Choose **Manually select features**. Then, use the **space** key and **arrow** keys to select different features as shown in Figure 65.

```
? Check the features needed for your project:
>(*) Babel
 ( ) TypeScript
 ( ) Progressive Web App (PWA) Support
 (*) Router
 (*) Vuex
 ( ) CSS Pre-processors
 (*) Linter / Formatter
 ( ) Unit Testing
 ( ) E2E Testing
```

Figure 65: Select features for the project

For **use history mode for router?** Set it to **n.** Next, you can select a linter and select the **ESLint + Standard config** option.

```
? Pick a linter / formatter config:
  ESLint with error prevention only
  ESLint + Airbnb config
> ESLint + Standard config
  ESLint + Prettier
```

Figure 66: Pick a linter/formatter config

Pick **Lint on save** as the next selection and save config files in dedicated config files.

```
? Pick additional lint features: (Press <space> to select, <a> to toggle all, <i> to invert selection)
>(*) Lint on save
 ( ) Lint and fix on commit
```

```
? Where do you prefer placing config for Babel, ESLint, etc.? (Use arrow keys)
> In dedicated config files
  In package.json
```

If you want, you can save this preset for later use. Once you have come to this point your project is finally created. In the terminal, change your current directory to the **my-quiz-ui** and you can build and run the project by running the following command. The website can be viewed on by navigating to the URL http://localhost:8000

```
$ npm run serve
```

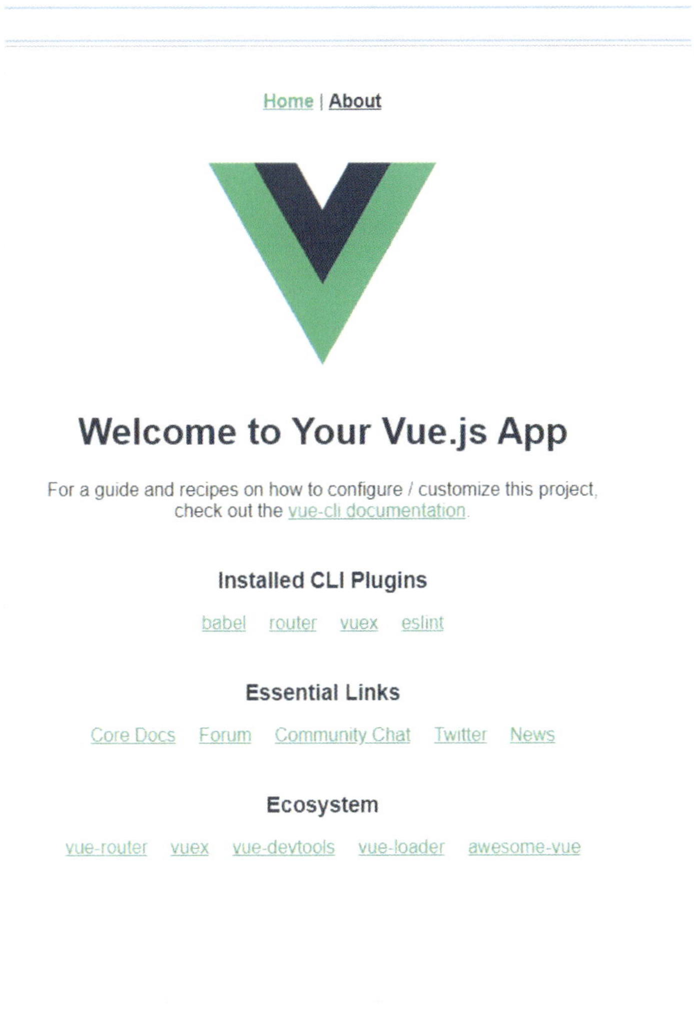

Home | About

Welcome to Your Vue.js App

For a guide and recipes on how to configure / customize this project,
check out the vue-cli documentation.

Installed CLI Plugins

babel   router   vuex   eslint

Essential Links

Core Docs   Forum   Community Chat   Twitter   News

Ecosystem

vue-router   vuex   vue-devtools   vue-loader   awesome-vue

Figure 67: How the website looks at the beginning

As this is not a book on Vue.js, we are not going to explain how Vue works here. However, if you are interested, you can find more information on https://cli.vuejs.org/

First commit to Azure Repos

Now we have a running application as shown in Figure 67. However, this is not exactly how we want our site to look like. Therefore, let us do some changes in the code to achieve something that we need.

Inside the component **HelloWorld.vue**, delete the HTML inside the first **<div>** under **<template>** tag, and add the code shown in Figure 68. (Although HelloWorld.vue is not a good starting file for the myQuiz project, let us keep it simple for now).

Figure 68: Helloworld.vue changed

Now, our web site looks something like below.

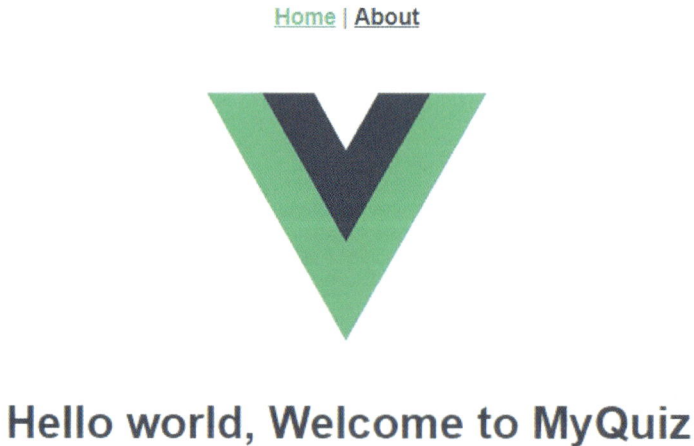

Figure 69: Welcome to MyQuiz heading

It is quite important that there is a **one-to-one** mapping between an application and a git repository. Now we have created our front-end part of the application. So, it is an isolated application and it needs to live in its own repository. So, navigate into the folder **my-quiz-ui** and you will see that it already has got a **.git** folder, which means it has been initialized as a local git repository. If you open a git bash terminal inside this folder you might see that you are currently in the **master** branch of your git repository.

```
milin@DESKTOP-EAHL5DR MINGW64 ~/OneDrive/Documents/Projects/MyQuiz/my-quiz-ui (master)
$ |
```

Figure 70: Master branch selected

If you type **git status**, you will see all your uncommitted changes. In this case, we changed only one file.

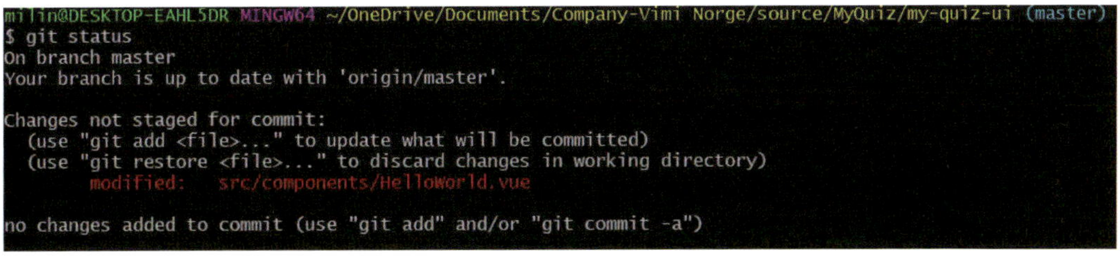

```
milin@DESKTOP-EAHL5DR MINGW64 ~/OneDrive/Documents/Company-Vimi Norge/source/MyQuiz/my-quiz-ui (master)
$ git status
On branch master
Your branch is up to date with 'origin/master'.

Changes not staged for commit:
  (use "git add <file>..." to update what will be committed)
  (use "git restore <file>..." to discard changes in working directory)
        modified:   src/components/HelloWorld.vue

no changes added to commit (use "git add" and/or "git commit -a")
```

Figure 71: Changes made so far

Add your changes to the staging area using the following command.

```
$ git add src/components/HelloWorld.vue
```

Now you can commit the change to your local **master** branch. When you commit, you can link the work item related to your commit. For example, the goal of our change is to add a heading to our web site. Suppose the related task for this change is "**12- Create a heading for the application**" as shown in Figure 72.

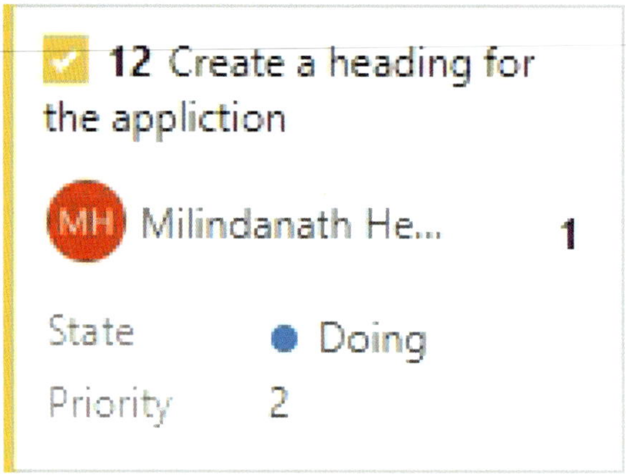

Figure 72: Work item related to the change

Write the following command with your **#task-number** and a meaningful message describing the change.

$ git commit -m "#12 Created a heading for the application"

Now we have successfully committed our first change to the local git repository. However, it is not available in Azure Repos yet, so that our team members can see it. In order to achieve that, let us create a brand-new repository in Azure Repos.

Click on the menu item **Repos** and select **New repository** in Azure DevOps as shown in Figure 73.

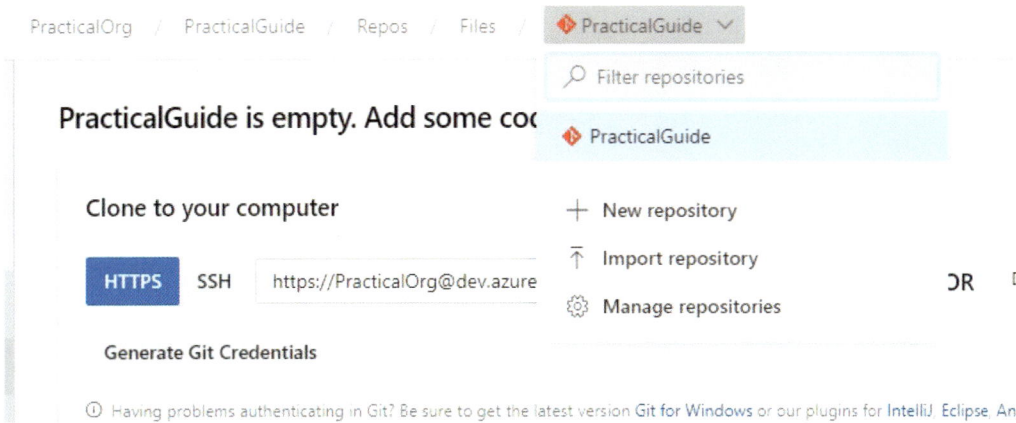

Figure 73: Create a new repository

Name it as **MyQuiz.UI**. Remember to uncheck the checkbox **Add a README** and click on the **Create** button.

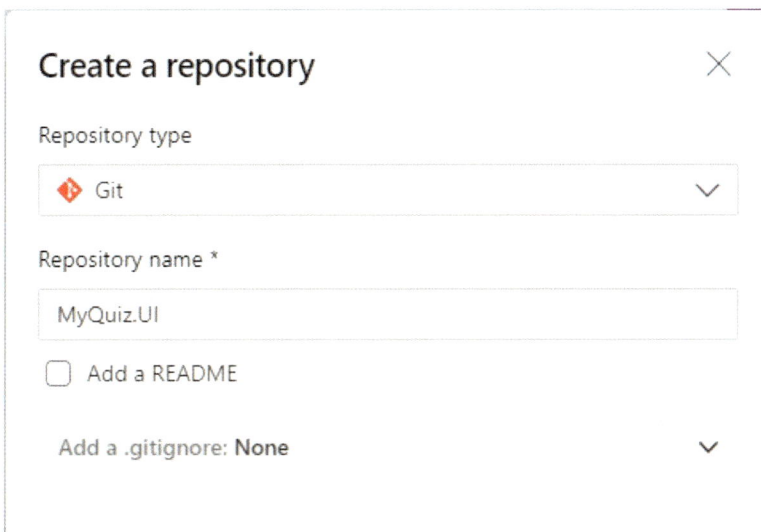

Figure 74: Create a new repository dialog

In order to push our application to the Azure DevOps remote repository, use the commands we discussed in the second option at the beginning of this chapter.

Push an existing repository from command line

HTTPS   SSH

git remote add origin
https://PracticalOrg@dev.azure.com/PracticalOrg/PracticalGuide/_git/MyQuiz.UI

Figure 75: Command to add an existing repository to Azure Repos

If you have not opened a Git Bash under the **my-quiz-ui** folder, then open it and paste these two commands you copied earlier one after the other. You have to probably authenticate yourself if you have not done so yet.

```
milin@DESKTOP-EAHL5DR MINGW64 ~/OneDrive/Documents/Projects/MyQuiz/my-quiz-ui (master)
$ git remote add origin https://PracticalOrg@dev.azure.com/PracticalOrg/PracticalGuide/_git/MyQuiz.UI

milin@DESKTOP-EAHL5DR MINGW64 ~/OneDrive/Documents/Projects/MyQuiz/my-quiz-ui (master)
$ git push -u origin --all
```

If everything goes well, you will see a different page in your Azure DevOps repos page, once you do a refresh. This is shown in Figure 76.

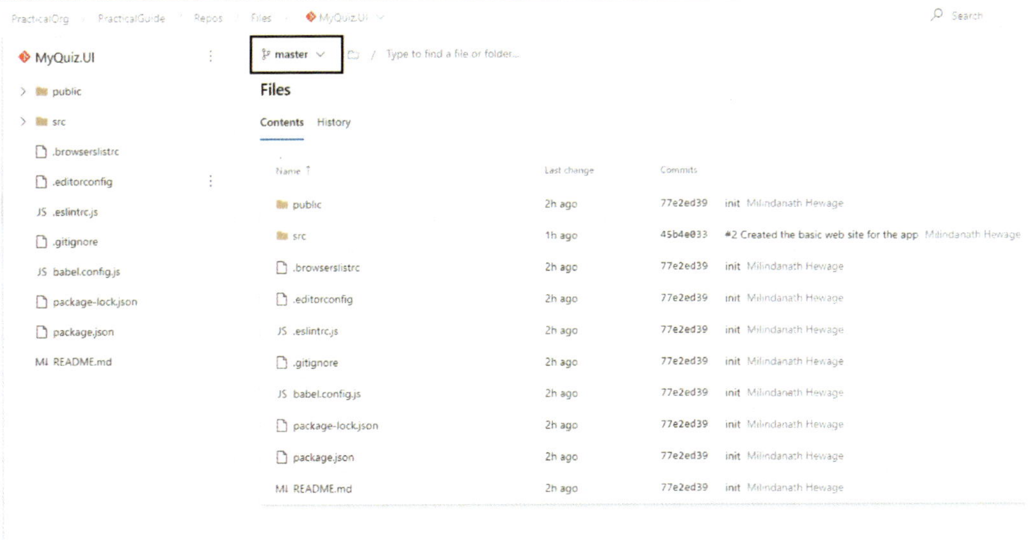

Figure 76: MyQuiz-UI repository after pushing the code changes

Remember that all your changes are pushed to the **master** branch of your repository. So, now we have successfully pushed our code to Azure DevOps Repos. Let us now look closer into each sub menu under **Repos** menu in Azure DevOps.

Files

Here, you can see the name of the project and all the files in a tree structure under that. You can also filter the results by the branch you need to see as shown in Figure 77. In addition to that, you can search for a specific file or a folder.

Figure 77: Top of the Files section

Contents tab is selected by default and you see the same file structure in the right-hand side as shown in Figure 78. You can also see the commits and when you did the last change.

Figure 78: File contents

In the **History** tab, you can see all your commits to the repository. For example, you can see the last commit we did for the task 12.

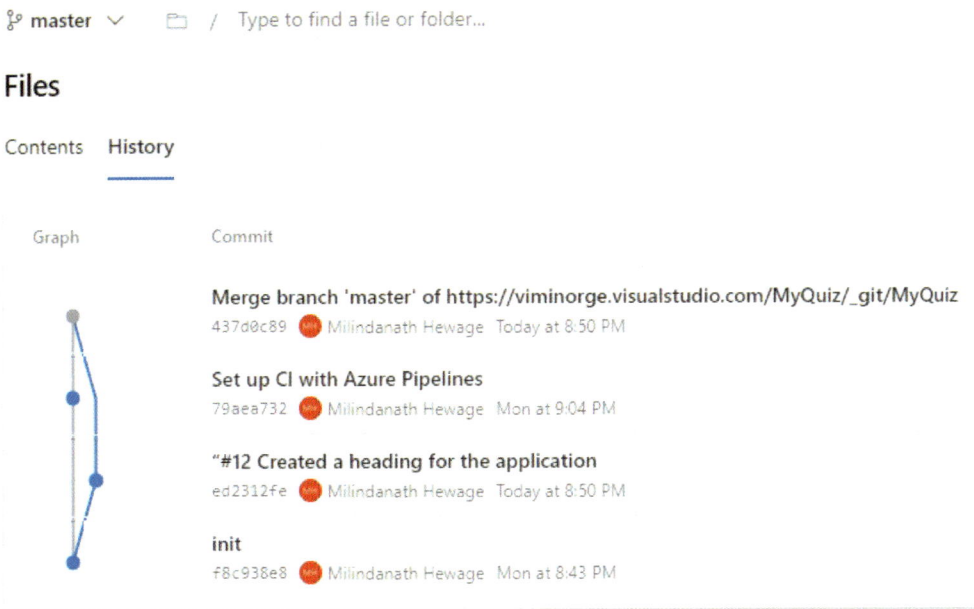

Figure 79: Commits history

If you remember when we committed the change, we added **#12** at the beginning of the commit message. Now, if you navigate to Azure Boards and navigate to task number 12, you will find a link to the commit. This can be very useful to link your code changes to the tasks you are working on.

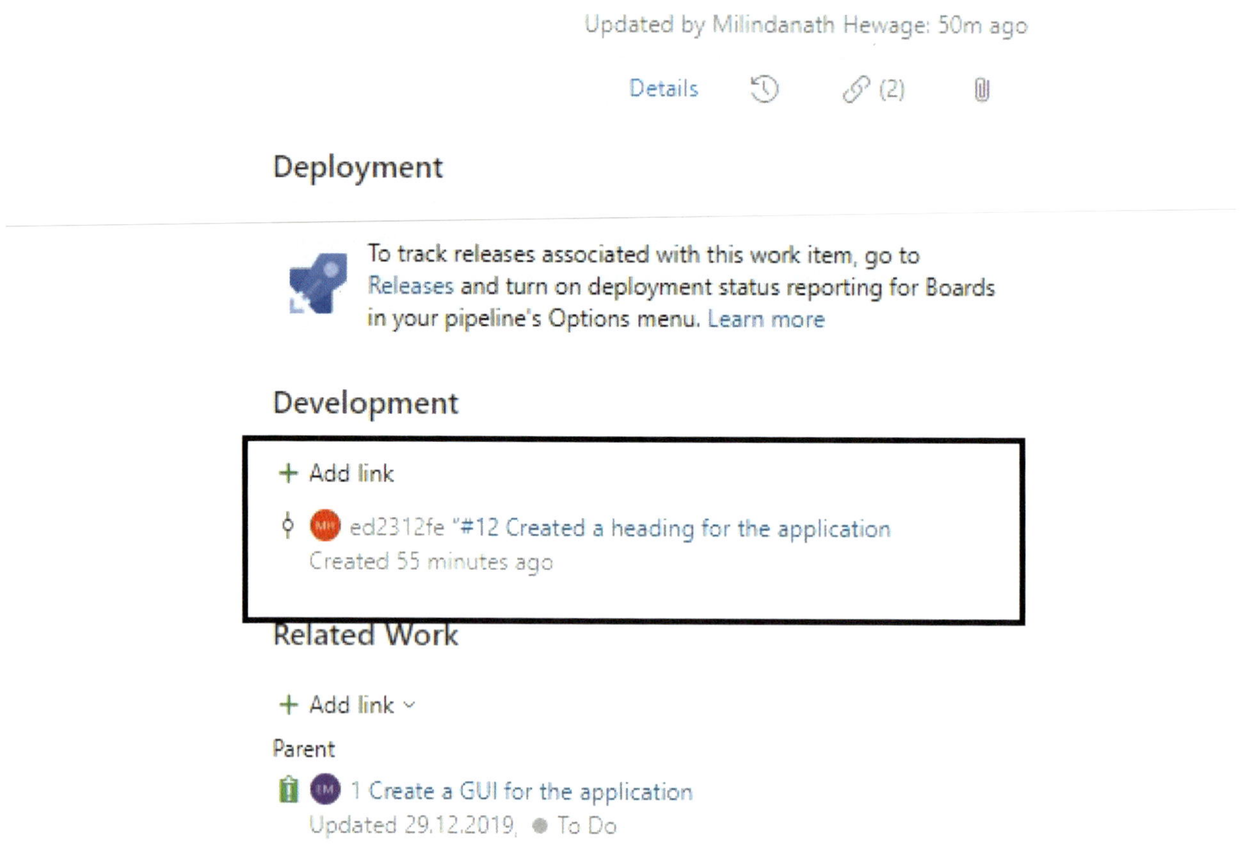

Updated by Milindanath Hewage: 50m ago

Details ⟲ 𝒮 (2) 📎

Deployment

To track releases associated with this work item, go to Releases and turn on deployment status reporting for Boards in your pipeline's Options menu. Learn more

Development

+ Add link

⚲ (MH) ed2312fe "#12 Created a heading for the application
Created 55 minutes ago

Related Work

+ Add link ⌄

Parent

📗 (1M) 1 Create a GUI for the application
Updated 29.12.2019, ● To Do

Figure 80: Link to the git commit related to the task

Commits

Under the commits section, you can see all the commits done to the whole repository. It shows a graphical view in addition to the commit messages as shown in Figure 81.

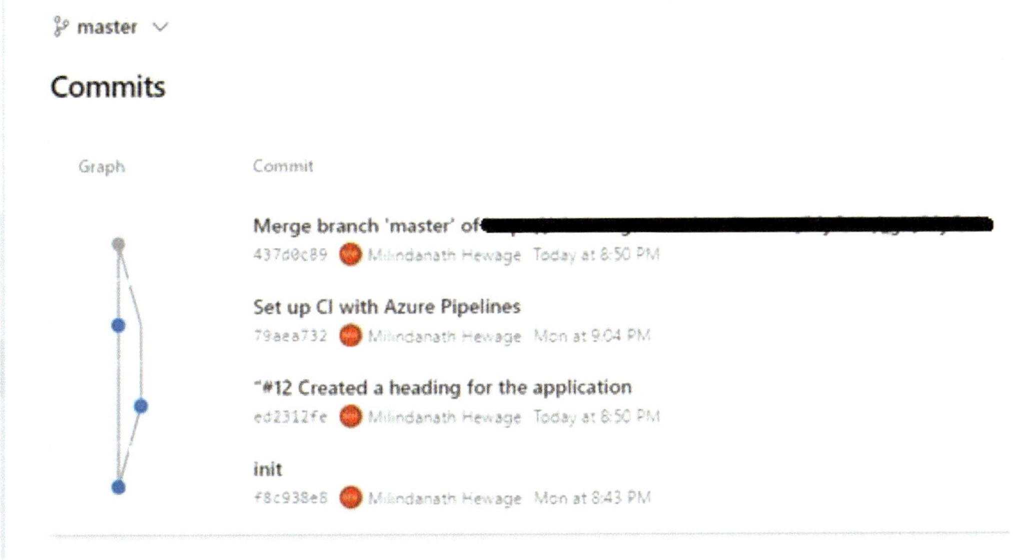

Figure 81: Commits to the repository

Pushes

Pushes section under Repos shows all the pushes you have done to the repository. If you expand a specific push, you can see all the commits related to that push.

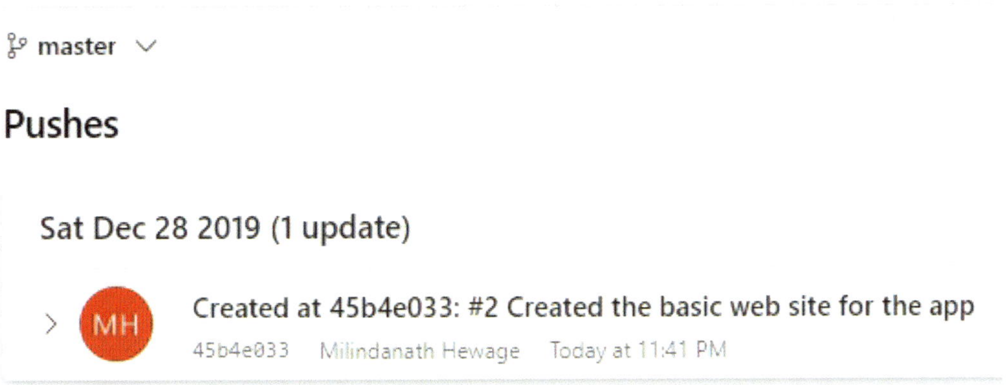

Figure 82: Pushes to the repository

Branches

When we are working in a team, we have to collaborate with other team members and share the code with each other. That is why we are using Azure Repos through Git repositories. Branches in Azure Repos provide a smooth way to achieve this.

We have already worked with the **master** branch in our previous examples. However, master branch itself is not enough for a better collaboration. Therefore, we need to create branches off the master branch to work on different work item tasks assigned to us through Azure Boards. To create a branch from the master, you can navigate to **Repos** -> **Branches** and click on the more icon on the right to get the context menu. Click on the link **New Branch**.

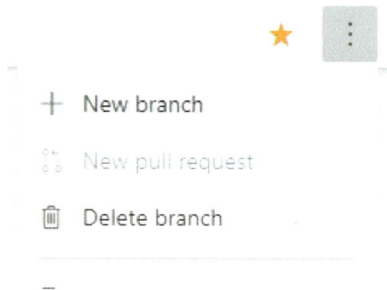

Figure 83: New branch from master

In the following modal dialog, give a **name** to your new branch, and select **master** as the "**Based on**" option. In addition to that, you can link a work item to this branch.

Create a branch

Name *

users/milindanath/13

Based on

⎇ master   ⌄

Work items to link   1   Clear all

Search work items by ID or title   ⌄

☑ Task 13: Possibility to create a new question   ✕
Updated Just now. ● To Do

Cancel   **Create**

Figure 84: Modal dialog for creating a branch

Then, click on the **Create** button to create you branch. The branch is created under the folder **users/milindanath** as shown in Figure 85.

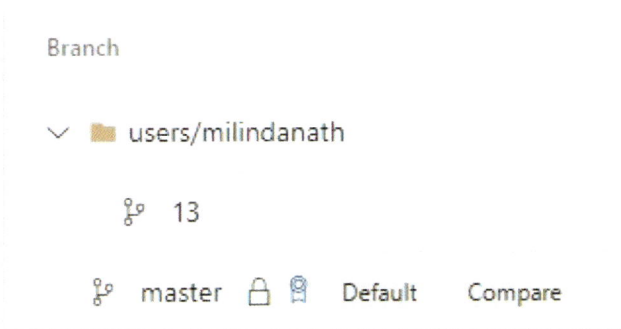

Branch

⌄ ■ users/milindanath

⎇   13

⎇ master 🔒 🎖 Default   Compare

Figure 85: New branch hierarchy

> Use a branch naming convention that matches your team. For example,
>   1. features/feature-id
>   2. users/username/feature-id
>   3. features/feature-name
>   4. bugfix/description
>   5. releases/release-number

We also need a suitable branching strategy based on the team and environment we work on. Basically, there are two well-known branching strategies used by teams.

Trunk-based branching

This is a very simple branching strategy with the following features.

1. **Master branch** is the central branch. (*Completed work*)
2. Create a **feature branch** from the **master** for all new features and bug fixes. (*Work in progress*)
3. **Merge** feature branches into the **master** branch using **pull requests**. (*Transition from Work in progress to Completed*)
4. Create a **release branch** from the **master** when you need to release a version of the code. (*Completed work goes to production*)
5. Create a **hotfix** branch from the master to fix critical production bugs. Merge the changes back to master, and use **git cherry-pick** command to bring back the changes into the release branch.

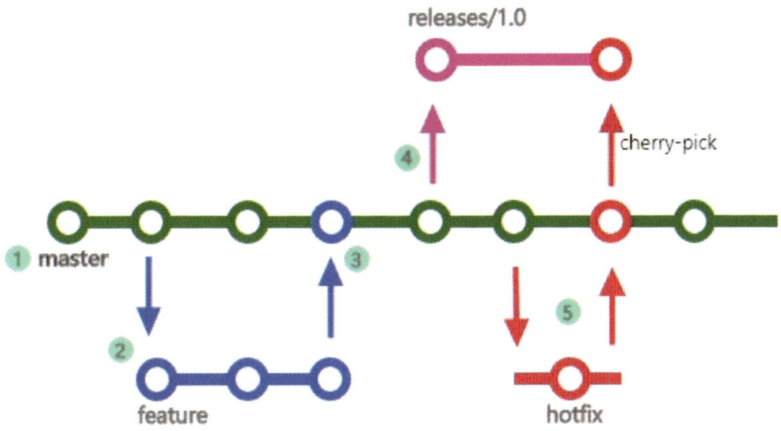

Figure 86: trunk-based branching strategy

The master branch requires to be kept up to date, and it needs to contain the latest code. In our previous example, we did our change directly on the master branch. However, in trunk-based scenario, it is not recommended to do so. Instead, you need to create a **feature branch**. For example, when we work on task 12, we can create a feature branch named **feature/12.** Now, the question is how we get the changes in the feature branch back into the master branch. The solution is to use pull requests (We will discuss more about pull requests in the next section). So, it is quite important that you do not allow the team members directly push their changes to the master branch. Instead, it should be done through pull requests. Let us see how we can lock the master branch for editing in Azure DevOps.

1. Navigate to **Repos -> Branches.**

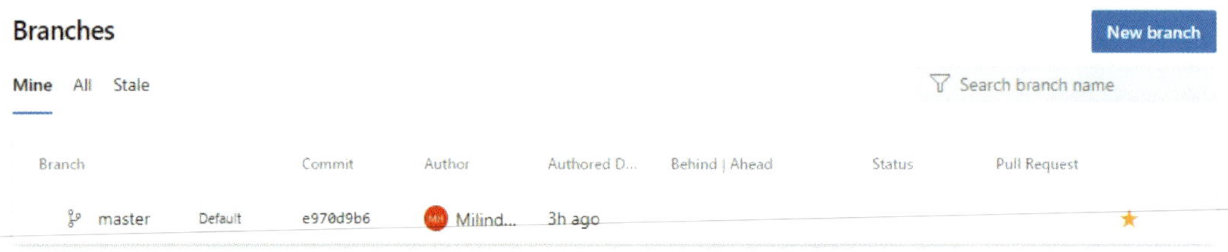
Branches
New branch
Mine
All
Stale
Search branch name
Branch
Commit
Author
Authored D...
Behind | Ahead
Status
Pull Request
master
Default
e970d9b6
Milind...
3h ago

Figure 87: master branch in the branches page

2. In the master branch, click on the more icon on the right-hand corner and select **branch policies**.

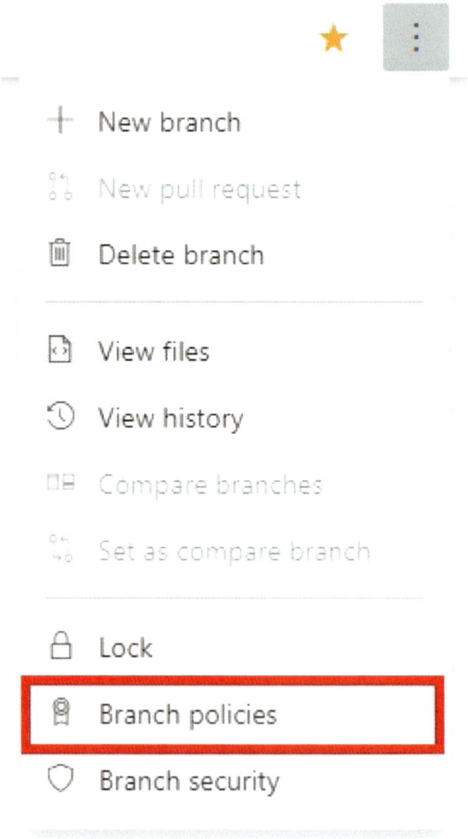
New branch
New pull request
Delete branch
View files
View history
Compare branches
Set as compare branch
Lock
Branch policies
Branch security

Figure 88: Select branch policies

3. Create at least one branch policy (For example, *Require a minimum number of reviewers*) in the following page so that you can prevent members directly pushing changes to the master branch.

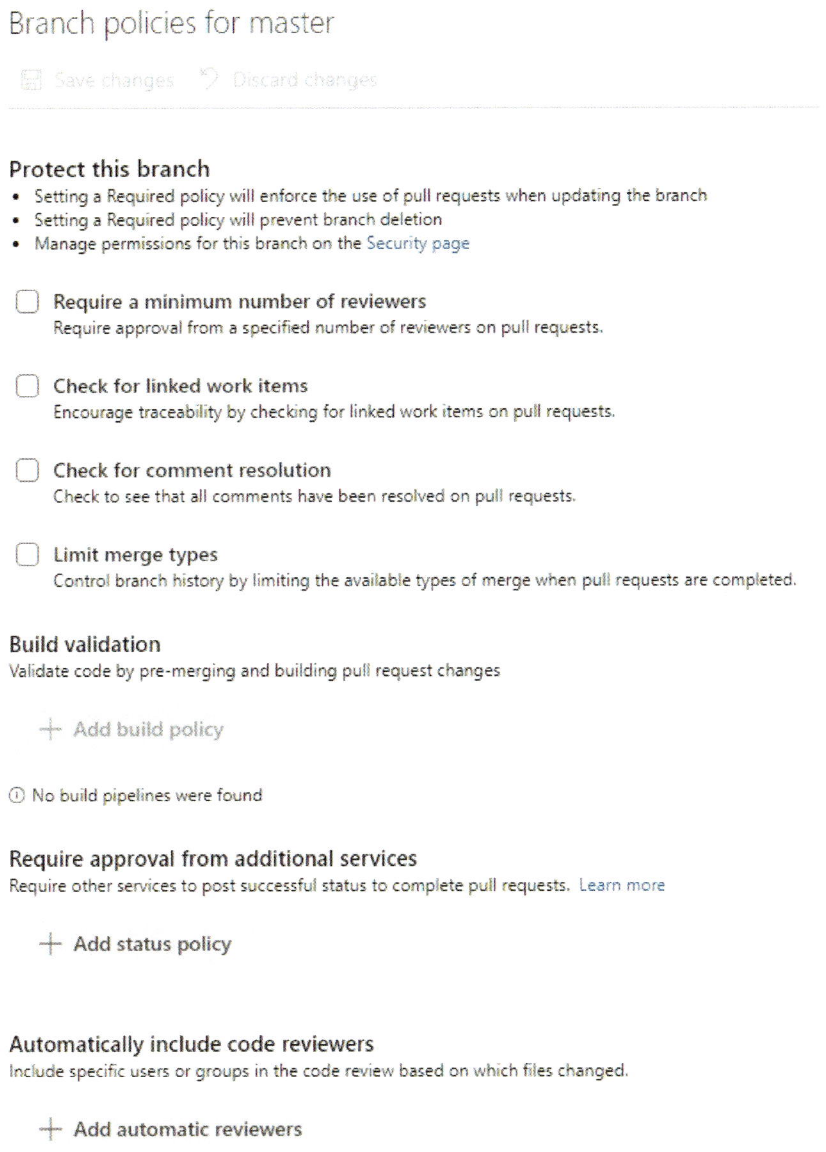

Branch policies for master

🖫 Save changes   ⤺ Discard changes

Protect this branch
- Setting a Required policy will enforce the use of pull requests when updating the branch
- Setting a Required policy will prevent branch deletion
- Manage permissions for this branch on the Security page

☐ **Require a minimum number of reviewers**
   Require approval from a specified number of reviewers on pull requests.

☐ **Check for linked work items**
   Encourage traceability by checking for linked work items on pull requests.

☐ **Check for comment resolution**
   Check to see that all comments have been resolved on pull requests.

☐ **Limit merge types**
   Control branch history by limiting the available types of merge when pull requests are completed.

Build validation
Validate code by pre-merging and building pull request changes

   ＋ Add build policy

ⓘ No build pipelines were found

Require approval from additional services
Require other services to post successful status to complete pull requests. Learn more

   ＋ Add status policy

Automatically include code reviewers
Include specific users or groups in the code review based on which files changed.

   ＋ Add automatic reviewers

Figure 89: Branch policies page

4. Now, let us check if we can edit any file in master branch. So, navigate to **Files** sub menu and open **src** -> **components** -> **HelloWorld.vue** page.

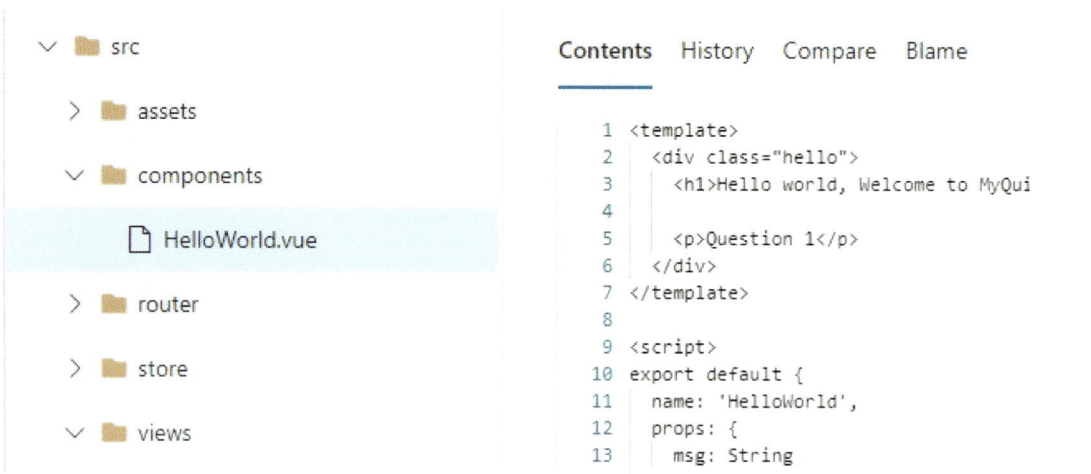

Figure 90: File contents

5. Click on the Edit button and do a small change in the file.

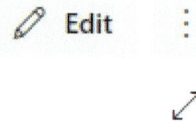

6. Now click on the **Commit** button.

7. Type in a **comment** and then click **Commit** again. Then you will see that you cannot commit any change to the master branch anymore.

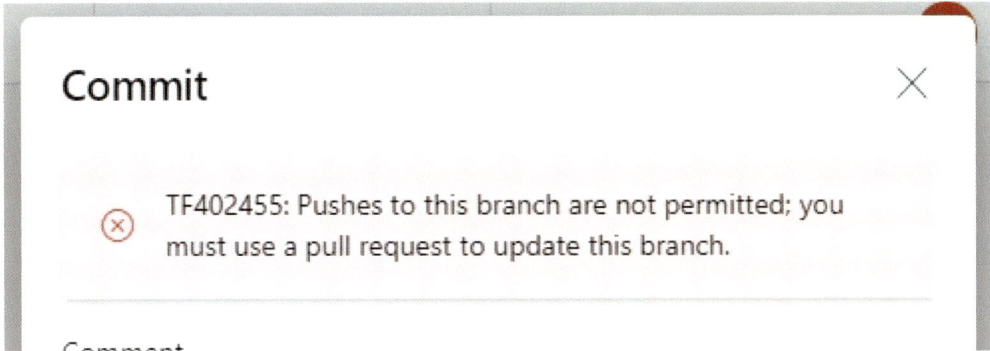

Commit ✕

TF402455: Pushes to this branch are not permitted; you must use a pull request to update this branch.

Figure 91: Error message about preventing pushes to the master branch

Git flow

Git flow uses a set of long running branches to represent different stages of the development cycle. The **master** branch always contains the stable code that is deployed (or will be deployed) to production. In addition to the master branch, there is a parallel branch called **develop** that is used by developers to work from. Developers can create their **feature** branches from the **develop** branch. Once the develop branch comes to a stable point, you can merge it to the master branch for the next release. This can be done through a release branch and the bug fixing on the release branch has to be continuously merged back into the develop branch. Once you are satisfied with the release branch, you can merge it to the master branch for the next release. Hotfixes to the current version can be done on a hotfix branch from master and merged back to both master and develop. This is shown in Figure 92.

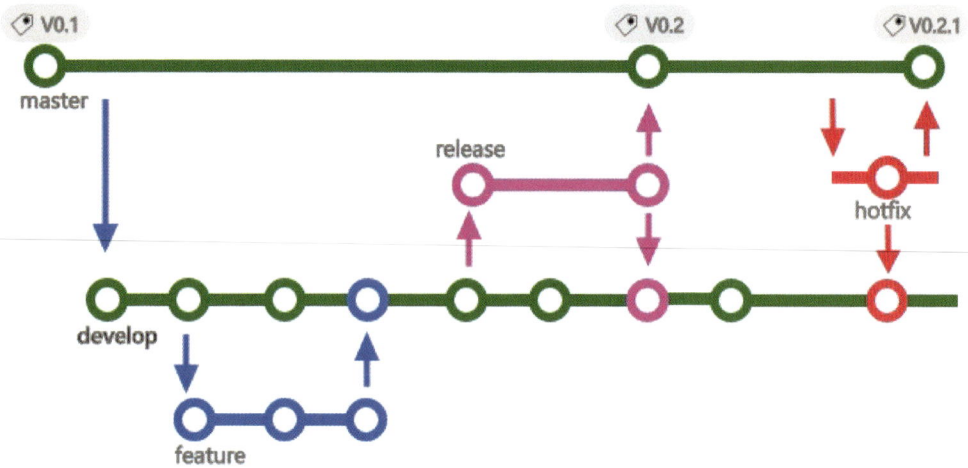

Figure 92: git flow branching strategy

As explained in the previous section, you can use pull requests to merge changes to **develop**, **release** and **master** branches.

Tags

Git tags are used to mark a specific commit as an important point in the history. Usually, this is used to mark a release point, at which commit a certain version of the code was released. However, you do not need to create tags if you are using release branches to manage your releases.

The easiest way to create a tag is by navigating to the **Commits** sub menu. Here, you go to a specific comment and click on the more icon on the right-hand corner.

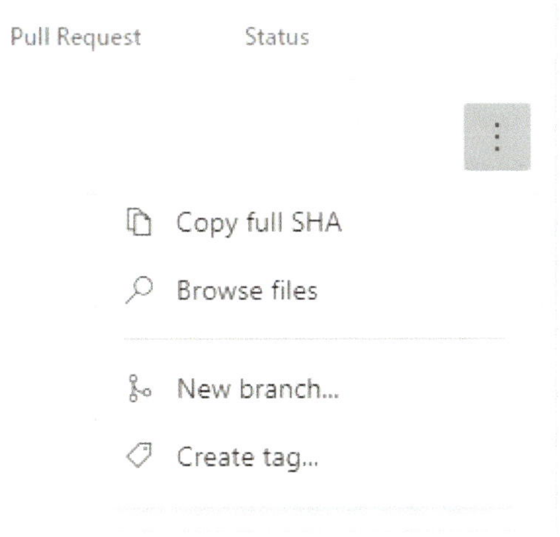

Figure 93: Create tag from the context menu

Now, click on the **Create tag** link. In the modal dialog, you can write a **name** and a **description** for your tag and click on the **Create** button.

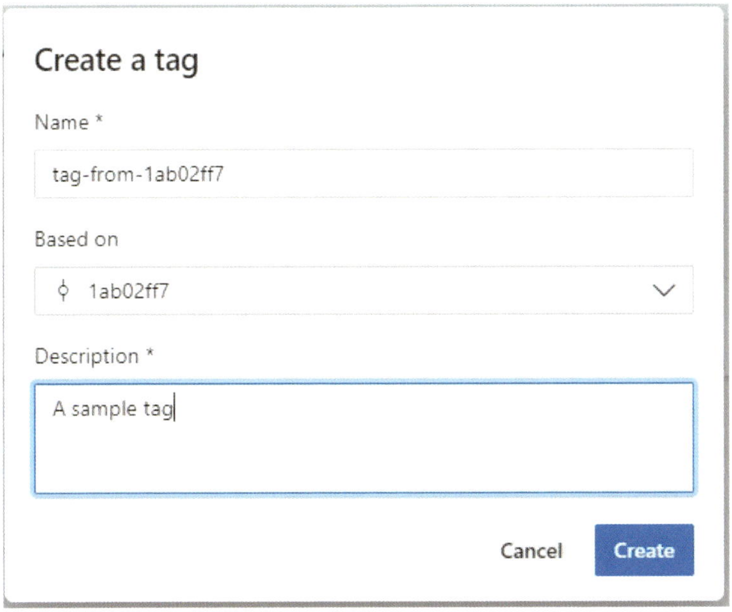

Figure 94: Modal dialog for creating a tag

Now, you will see a new tag is created with the whole source code of the project.

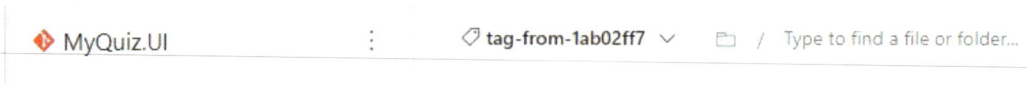

Figure 95: Tag created

Moreover, you will see a label attached to the commit you created the tag for.

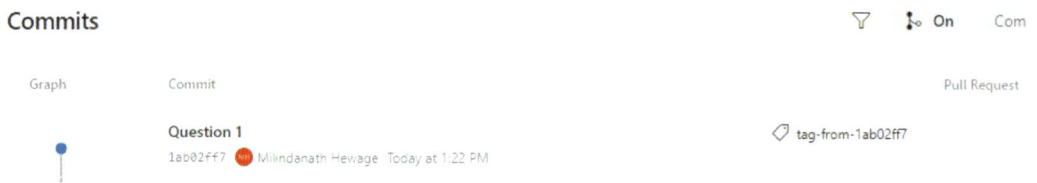

Figure 96: commit related to the tag

You can see all the tags created for your project by navigating to the **Tags** sub menu.

Figure 97: Tags list page

In order to edit the source code in a tagged version, you have to create a branch from the tag and then do a pull request to bring the changes back to the master.

Pull requests

Pull requests is a very good way of maintaining a high quality in your code. This allows you to discuss, review and quality assure your code changes before they get merged into your base branch. Pull requests functionality can be enabled to branches by setting branch policies. Let us see how we can use pull requests to our master branch. Open branch policies page for the master branch.

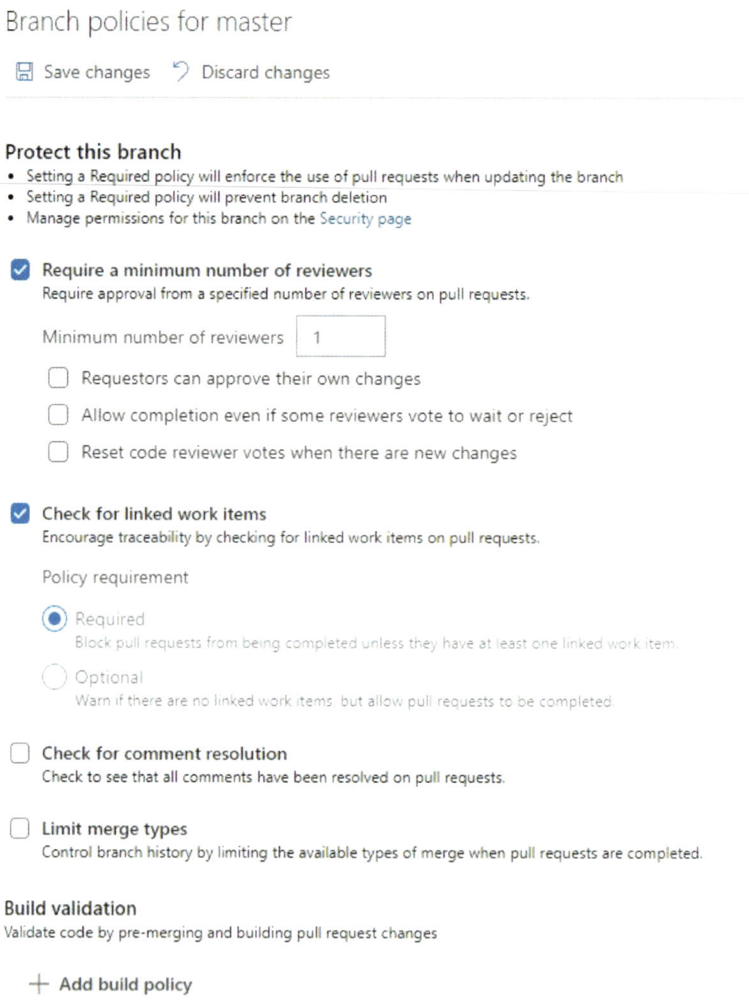

Branch policies for master

🖫 Save changes   ⤺ Discard changes

Protect this branch
- Setting a Required policy will enforce the use of pull requests when updating the branch
- Setting a Required policy will prevent branch deletion
- Manage permissions for this branch on the Security page

☑ **Require a minimum number of reviewers**
Require approval from a specified number of reviewers on pull requests.

Minimum number of reviewers   [1]

☐ Requestors can approve their own changes

☐ Allow completion even if some reviewers vote to wait or reject

☐ Reset code reviewer votes when there are new changes

☑ **Check for linked work items**
Encourage traceability by checking for linked work items on pull requests.

Policy requirement

◉ Required
Block pull requests from being completed unless they have at least one linked work item.

◯ Optional
Warn if there are no linked work items, but allow pull requests to be completed.

☐ **Check for comment resolution**
Check to see that all comments have been resolved on pull requests.

☐ **Limit merge types**
Control branch history by limiting the available types of merge when pull requests are completed.

Build validation
Validate code by pre-merging and building pull request changes

+ **Add build policy**

Figure 98: Set branch policies for the master branch

Here, you can add some restrictions and checks before a certain pull request can be accepted. For example,

1. Specify the number of reviewers who will review the code. You can also add an automatic code reviewer.
2. The application has to be built successfully in order to complete the pull request.
3. At least one work item has to be linked to the pull request.

Suppose we have set up our branch policy as shown in Figure 98. Now, let us try to work on a task and do some code changes.

1. Create a branch from your master branch with the name **feature/13**
2. Add some changes to your HelloWorld.vue file.
3. Commit and push those changes to the Azure Repos branch
4. Now, you can go to the Repos and to your branch **feature/13**. Then you will see the following message.

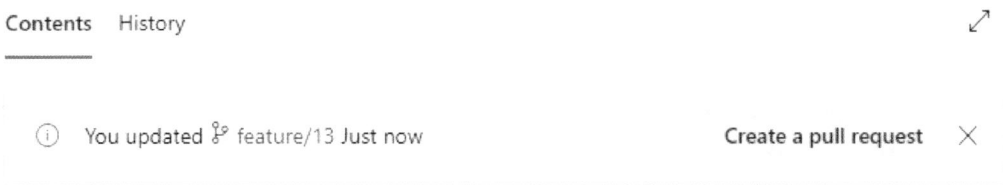

Contents   History   ↗

⟳   You updated ⅋ feature/13 Just now   Create a pull request   ✕

Figure 99: Create a pull request message

5. Click on the **Create a pull request** button to create the pull request
6. In the following page you can see that the pull request is from **feature/13** into **master** branch. You can also provide a suitable title and description for the pull request. Then add who is going to review your code. If you have not linked a task in your commit message, then do it here. After you fill all the required information, click on the Create button to start the pull request.

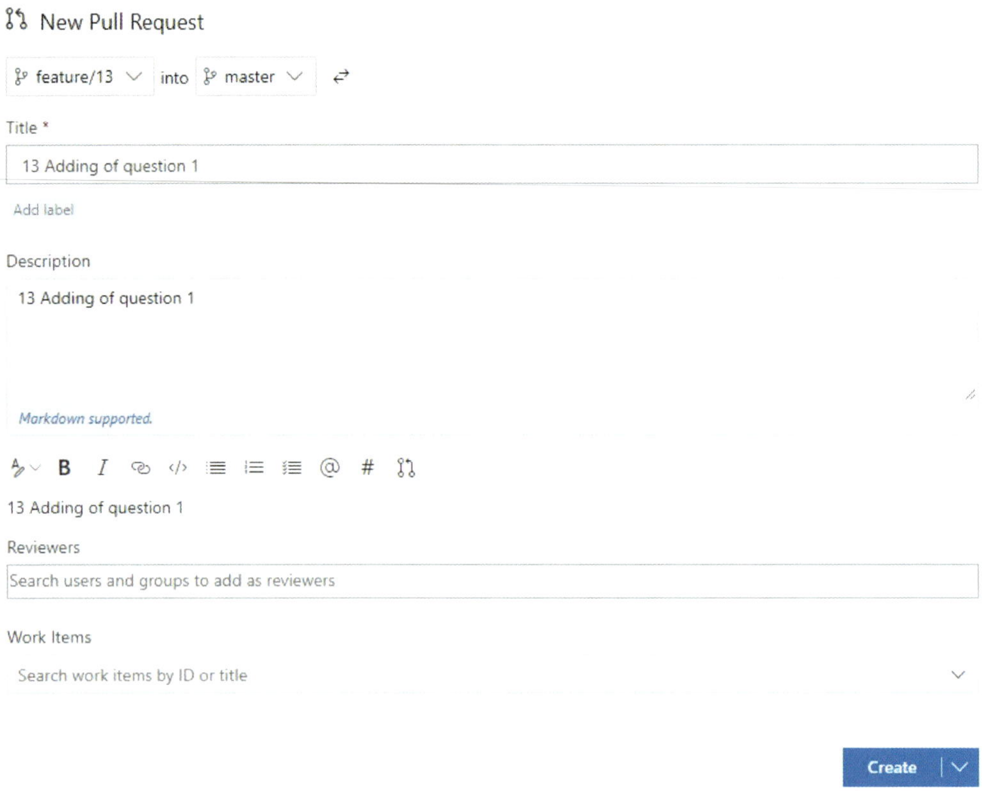

New Pull Request

feature/13 ∨ into master ∨ ⇄

Title *

13 Adding of question 1

Add label

Description

13 Adding of question 1

Markdown supported.

A∨ **B** *I* ⊘ </> ≡ ≔ ≔ @ # ⸜⸝

13 Adding of question 1

Reviewers

Search users and groups to add as reviewers

Work Items

Search work items by ID or title ∨

Create | ∨

Figure 100: New pull request page

7. If you do not specify a reviewer and a work item, then you will see that you have violated the branch policies as below.

Policies

Required
✗   0 of 1 reviewers approved
✗   No work items linked

Work Items   ✕   ＋

No related work items

Reviewers   ✉   ＋

No reviewers

Labels

Add label

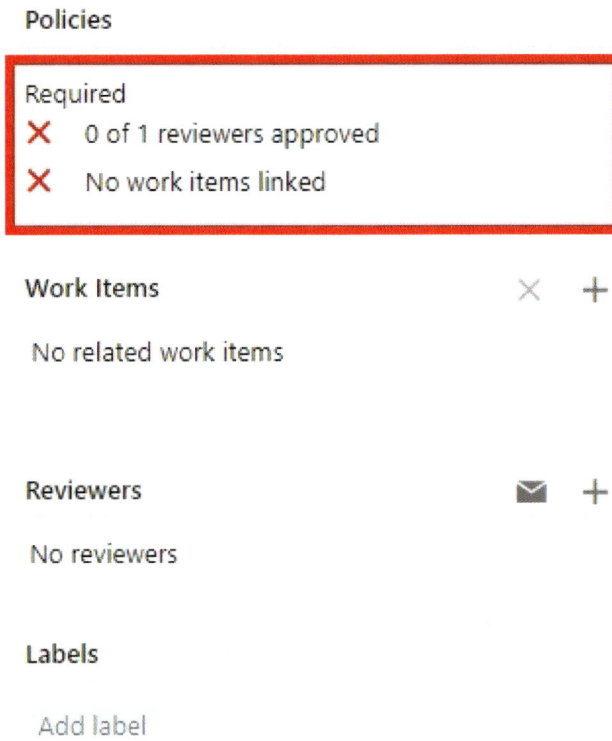

Figure 101: Branch policies not fulfilled yet

8. Even here you can add that information by clicking on the + sign.
9. In addition to that, the reviewers can start a conversation with the developer by adding comments in the comments section.

MH   Add a comment...

MH   Milindanath Hewage joined as a reviewer   just now

Created by MH Milindanath Hewage   2 minutes ago

Figure 102: Comments section in the pull request

10. Once you click on the **Files** tab, you can see the changes related to the pull request. Here, the reviewer can add comments at specific lines in the file.

Figure 103: Add comment to a file

11. Then you can start the conversation with the developer mentioning your concerns about the code. In this way, the team members can communicate back and forth to produce a high-quality code.

```
+        <h2>Question 1: Who is the founder of Microsoft?</h2>
+
+        <div>A: Bill Gates</div>
```

> **MH** This should be clickable and add a checkbox to
> select.
>
> *Markdown supported. Drag & drop, paste, or select files to insert.*

$A_{\vee}$ **B** *I* · · ·   **Comment**   Cancel

This should be clickable and add a checkbox to select.

```
+        <div>B: Satya Nadella</div>
+        <div>C: Steve Jobs</div>
+        <div>D: Mark Zuckerberg</div>
     </div>
   </template>
```

Figure 104: Add comments to specific portions of the code

12. Then, the developer can fix issues mentioned in the comment on the same branch and push the changes back to the server. Then, the new commit will appear under the pull request. You can also **Resolve** the comment added by the reviewer.

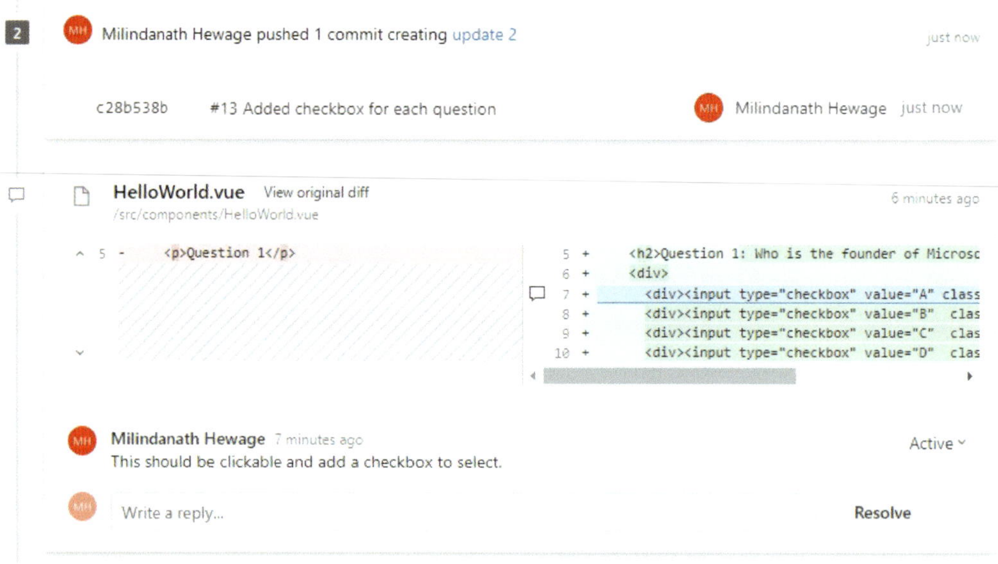

Figure 105: New commit that resolves the reviewer's suggestion

13. Once both the parties have agreed on the changes, the reviewer can approve the change by clicking on the **Approve** button.

14. Now, you will see that all the required branch policies are fulfilled. Click on the **Complete** button to finally start **merging** the code changes to master branch.

15. You can add a comment if you wish and set which merge type you want to merge the changes. Also, you can delete the feature branch after merge and set the work item to **Done** state.

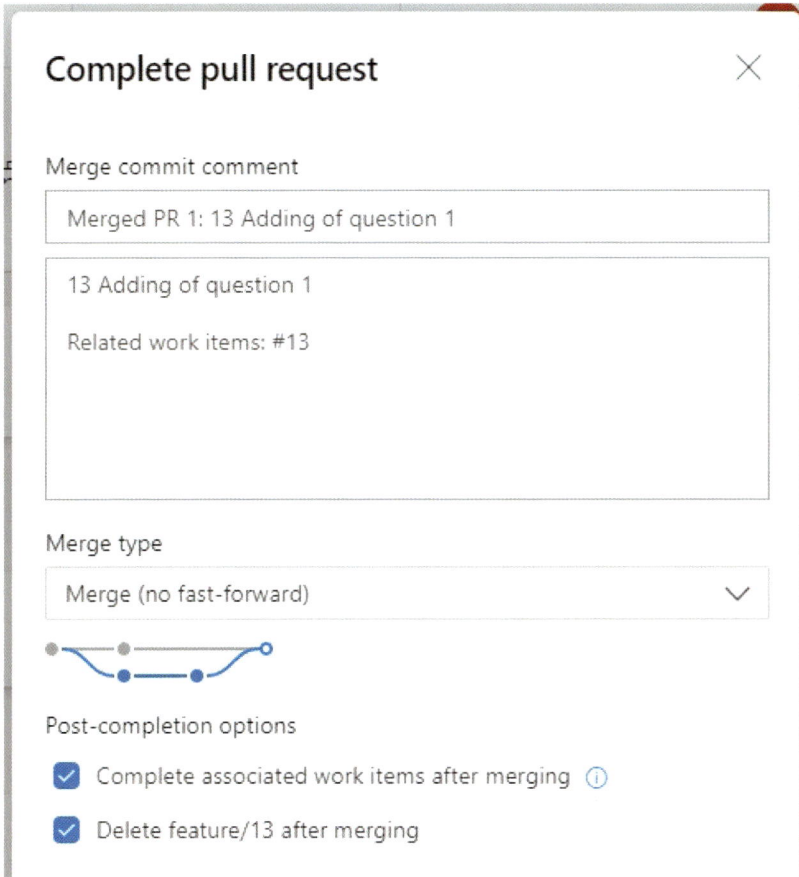

Figure 106: Complete pull request dialog

16. You will see a message saying that you have completed the pull request.

Figure 107: Pull request completed message

17. You can verify that your changes are committed to the master branch, by inspecting the commits to the master.

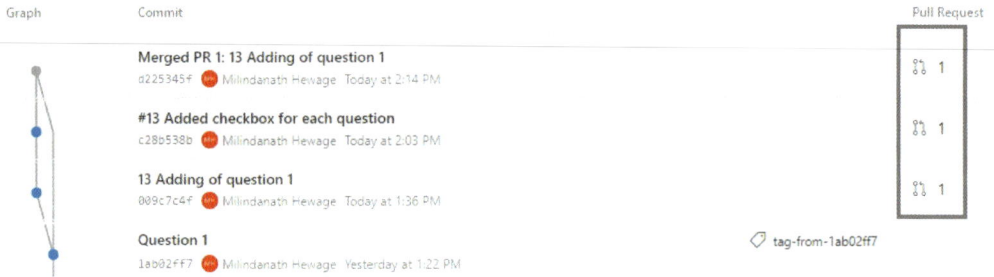

Figure 108: Commits related to the pull request

Summary

In this chapter, we learned about creating an application and moving its source code to a git repository located in Azure Repos. We also looked into different methods of creating a git repository in Azure Repos. Moreover, we learned about different parts of Azure Repos, such as Files, Commits, Pushes, Branches, Tags and pull requests.

Chapter 5
Azure Pipelines

Once you have pushed your code to Azure Repos, you can create a build pipeline and a release pipeline using Azure Pipelines. This is also known as Continuous Integration (CI) and Continuous Delivery (CD). Build pipeline (CI pipeline) allows you to automate the build and test process of your application. You can setup a build pipeline so that it builds and tests the application code each time a developer commits a change to the source code. The release pipeline (CD pipeline), with the help of the output of the build pipeline, allows you to automate the release process and continuously deliver a high-quality product to your customers.

Continuous Integration (CI)

Creating a build pipeline is the first step of Azure Pipelines. There are basically two ways you can start creating a build pipeline.

Method 1: Navigate to your repository by clicking on **Repos** and click on the **Set up build** button. In this option, you can skip the selection of the source code location as you are already inside the myquiz repository.

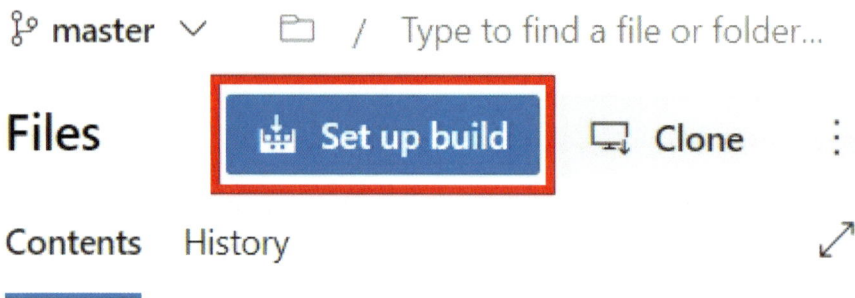

Figure 109: Set up build button

Method 2: Click on the menu item **Pipelines** on the left-hand side and then click on the button **Create Pipeline.**

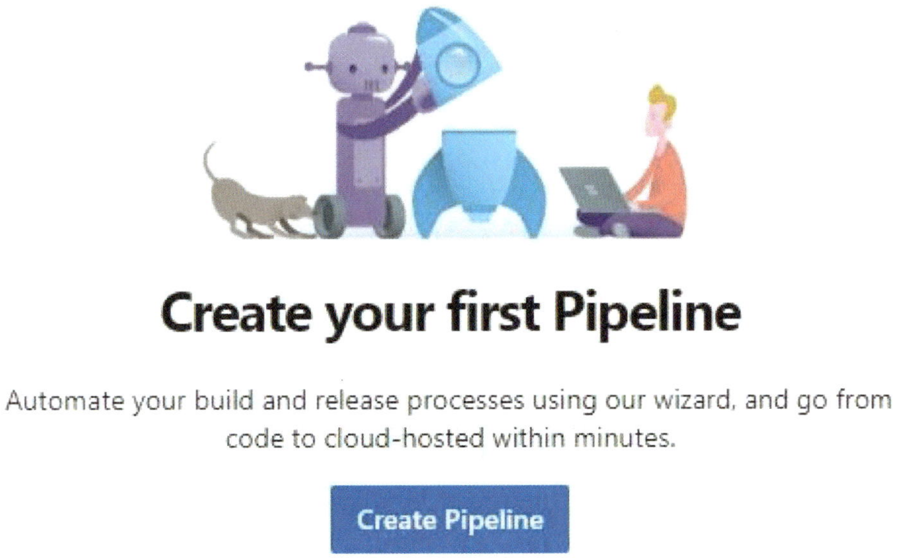

Figure 110: Create Pipeline page

If you choose **Method 2,** you have to specify where your source code resides. In this example, our source code resides in **Azure Repos Git**. Therefore, select **Azure Repos Git (YAML)** option as shown in Figure 111.

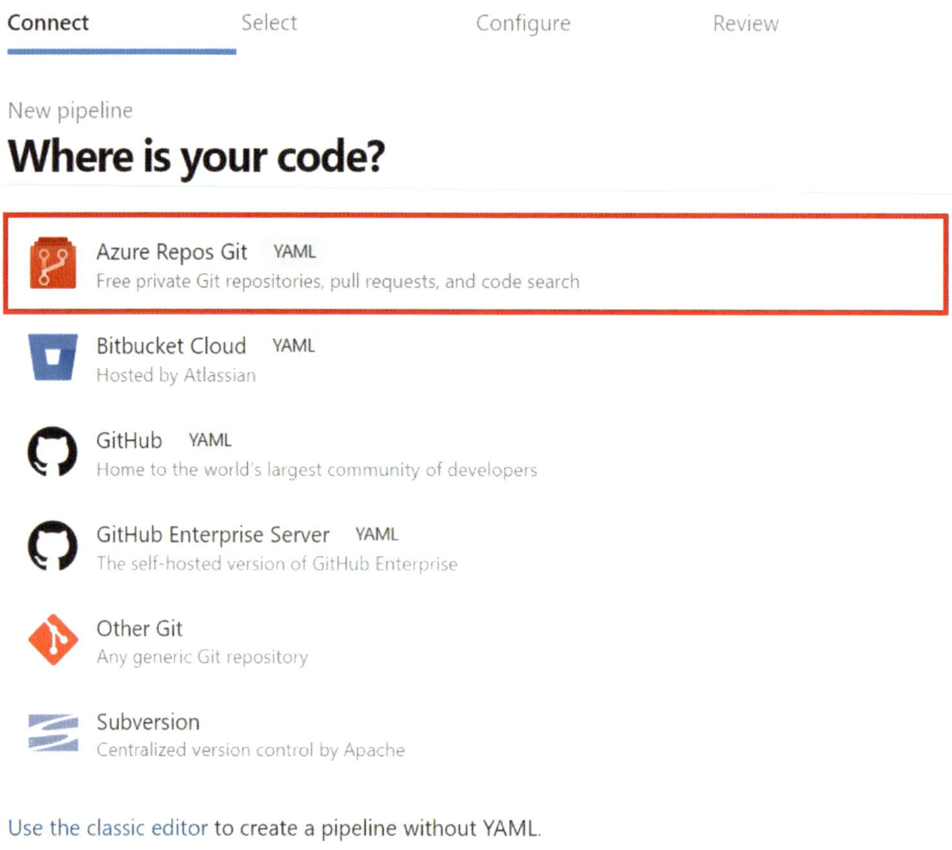

Connect   Select   Configure   Review

New pipeline

Where is your code?

Azure Repos Git   YAML
Free private Git repositories, pull requests, and code search

Bitbucket Cloud   YAML
Hosted by Atlassian

GitHub   YAML
Home to the world's largest community of developers

GitHub Enterprise Server   YAML
The self-hosted version of GitHub Enterprise

Other Git
Any generic Git repository

Subversion
Centralized version control by Apache

Use the classic editor to create a pipeline without YAML.

Figure 111: Select version control location

Next, you select your code repository. Select **MyQuiz.UI** that we created in the previous chapter.

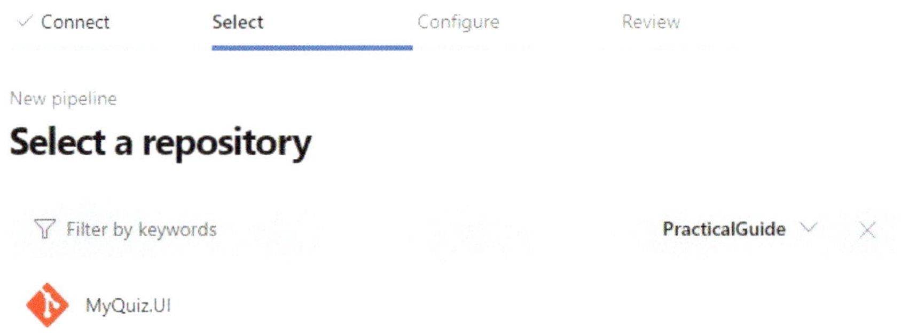

Figure 112: Select repository

Then you can configure your pipeline to match the technology you have selected to build your application. As we have built our application in Vue and Node.js, we select **Node.js with Vue** option.

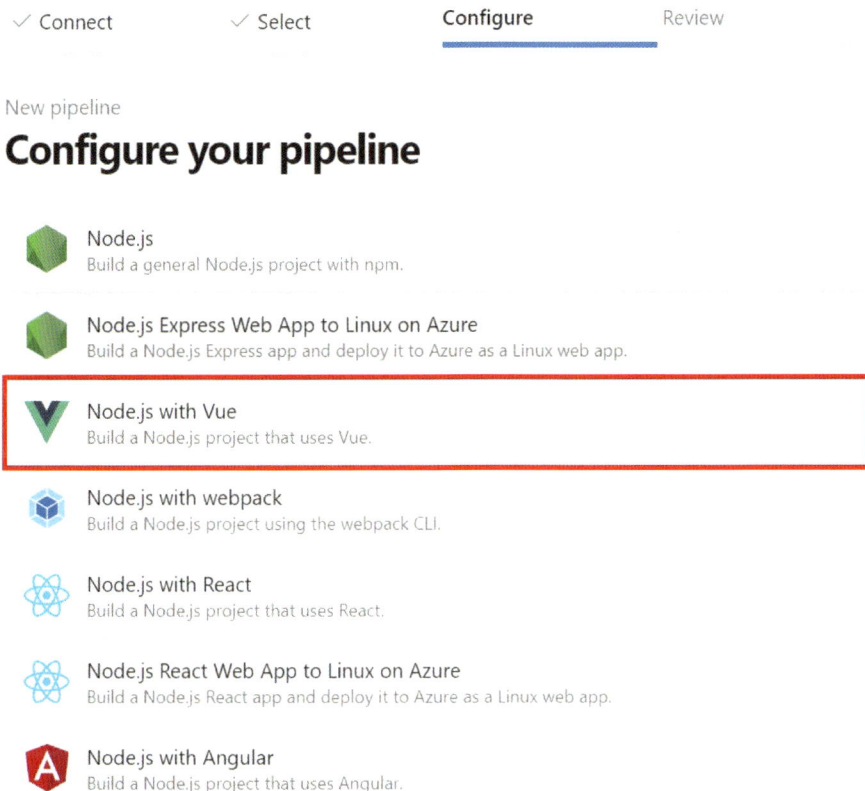

Figure 113: Configure pipeline for Node.js with Vue

Based on this selection, Azure pipelines creates a basic starting pipeline definition in YAML that matches Vue.js and Node. You can see the created **azure-pipelines.yml** file in Figure 114.

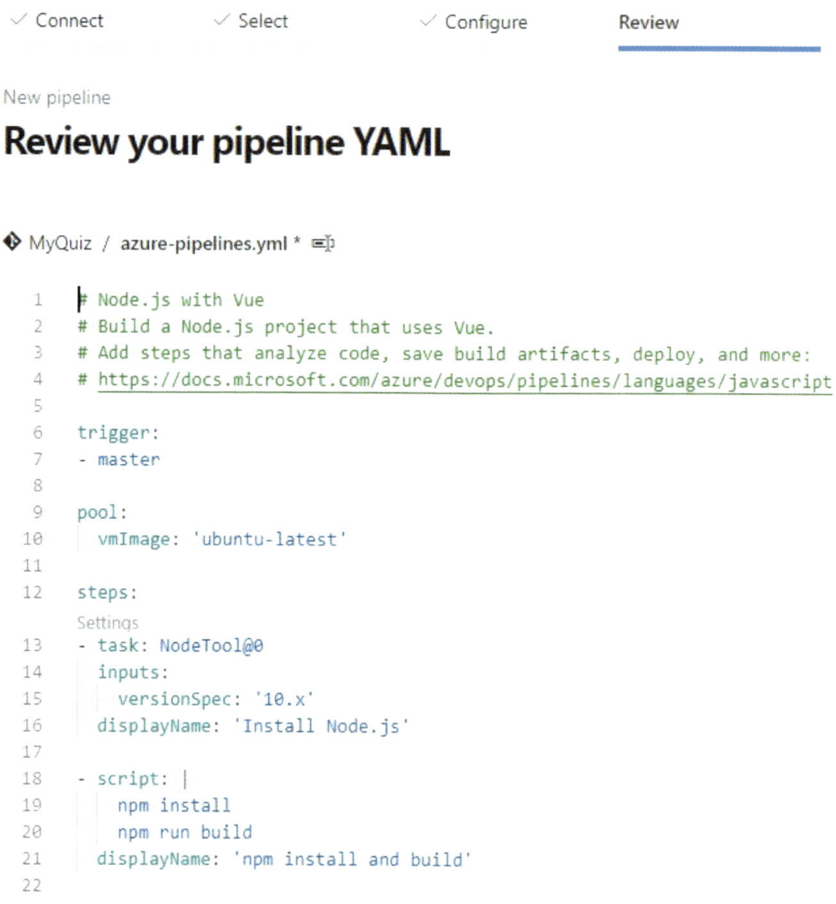

Figure 114: Basic pipeline definition file

In order to understand this file, we need some knowledge about YAML data serialization language. Let us try to understand the YAML syntax.

Introduction to YAML,

YAML (**YAML** Ain't Markup Language) is a data serialization language that is used by Azure pipelines to describe different commands in the pipeline. In other words, you define your build pipeline in code. The language is quite similar to JSON (JavaScript Object Notation) and represented in key value pairs. However, you need to pay attention to the correct indentation when writing YAML and use spaces for indentation. Two space indentation is recommended [4]. YAML files have the extension ".yaml" or ".yml". Let us look into a simple example to understand the YAML syntax.

Suppose we want to represent a person's data in YAML, and the person object has following attributes.

- *name* (string),
- *age* (integer),
- *marital status* (Boolean),
- *favourite sports* (array) and
- *contact details* (a structure that has a certain format).

We could write this information in YAML as in the following.

person:

  name: 'Mark Henry'

  age: 25

  married: true

  favourite_sports:

     – Football
     – Cycling
     – Swimming

  contact: |

    (+47) 12345679
    abcde@gmail.com

key: *value* pairs are the basic building blocks. value can come in different types. For example object, array, string, numbers, Boolean etc..

- = item in an array

| = preserve the formatting exactly as it is

Structure of the basic build definition

Using this syntax, let us try to understand the .yml build pipeline. Consider the first key-value pair.

```
trigger:
- master
```

According to what we have learned; this represents an **array**. In other words, an array of triggers. Basically, we want to trigger our build pipeline each time a developer checks in new code changes to the **master** branch. Assume, you want to run the build pipeline on all the release branches located under the **releases** folder, then you can modify this as follows.

```
trigger:
- master
- releases/*
```

If you want the build pipeline to kick off on every commit in every branch, then you can set it as follows.

```
trigger:
- '*'
```

Let's move on to the next command which defines the build agent pool.

```
pool:
  vmImage: 'ubuntu-latest'
```

In this command, it specifies a **Microsoft-hosted agent pool**. In Azure Pipelines, the name of this pool is *Azure Pipelines*. An agent pool is used to organize build agents.

Agent pool

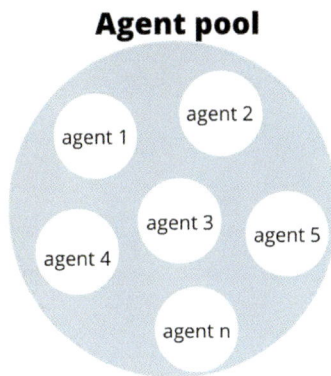

A **build agent** can be considered as the heart of the build pipeline, which performs all the jobs defined in the build pipeline. In an Azure DevOps services context, it is an installable software, which is hosted in a virtual machine.

As you can see, the **pool** object contains the **vmImage** property which contains the value '**ubuntu-latest**'. This means that we want to run our build pipeline in a build agent hosted in an Ubuntu virtual machine. **Azure pipelines hosted pool** gives you the option to select from several virtual machine images.

Table 1: Azure Pipelines hosted VM images

Virtual machine image	YAML label
Windows Server 2019 with Visual Studio 2019	**windows-latest** OR **windows-2019**
Windows Server 2016 with Visual Studio 2017	**vs2017-win2016**
Ubuntu 18.04	**ubuntu-latest** OR **ubuntu-18.04**
Ubuntu 16.04	**ubuntu-16.04**
macOS X Mojave 10.14	**macOS-latest** OR **macOS-10.14**

> You can also create a self-hosted agent if you prefer or if you are using on-premise builds using Azure DevOps server.

For example, if you want to run your build agent on a Windows Server 2019 machine having Visual Studio 2019, then you can change the yaml file as following.

```
pool:
  vmImage: 'windows-latest'
```

> A fresh virtual machine instance will be created in the Azure cloud each time you run your build pipeline and it will be discarded after the build process is completed.

The next set of commands define a **job** containing a series of steps performed by the agent. These steps are all about building the application.

```
steps:
- task: NodeTool@0
  inputs:
    versionSpec: '10.x'
  displayName: 'Install Node.js'

- script: |
    npm install
    npm run build
  displayName: 'npm install and build'
```

There are two steps defined here. The first one is a task to install node.js 10.x on the VM image. If you click on the **Settings** link on top of steps, you can see a graphical view of the task which gives you the possibility to add options to various inputs.

← Node.js tool installer

Version Spec * ⓘ

10.x

☐ Check for Latest Version ⓘ

Figure 115: Node.js tool installer task

Another way to achieve the same task is by adding a **demands** attribute to the agent pool. Here, you say that you want node package manager, installed on the agent machine.

```
pool:
  vmImage: 'ubuntu-latest'
  demands:
  - npm
```

The second task use *npm install* command to install the node packages and create a production build of our application using *npm run build* command. The pipe (|) symbol is used to preserve the formatting of two commands.

> *npm run build* **command** will build our application and creates a folder called *dist* under the root folder. Contents of the *dist* folder will be used when deploy our application to the production.

Extend the build pipeline

Now we have an understanding about the default yaml pipeline. Let us try to extend this by adding our own tasks to the steps list. What we are missing here is a way to package the build output into an artifact which we can use to deploy our application.

The bottom line is that your artifact should be copied into the artifact staging directory (represented by the variable *$(Build.ArtifactStagingDirectory)*) so that we can deploy it to production environment. The build output will be copied to the **dist** folder in the sources directory (represented by the variable *$(Build.SourcesDirectory) or $(System.DefaultWorkingDirectory)*).

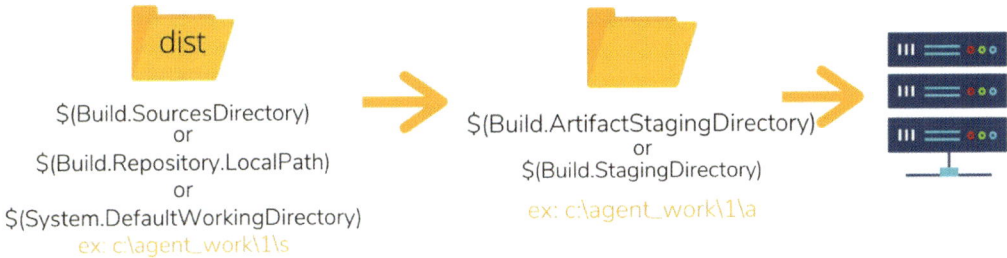

Copy files

There are basically three tasks associated for this step. First, you have to copy your **dist** folder to the **artifiact staging directory** (represented by the Azure variable *$(Build.ArtifactStagingDirectory)*) in Azure pipelines. Search for the **Copy files task** in the assistant section as shown in Figure 116.

Tasks   →⊡

🔍 copy files|

⊡ **Azure file copy**
Copy files to Azure Blob Storage or virtual machin...

⊡ **Copy files**
Copy files from a source folder to a target folder ...

⊡ **Copy files over SSH**
Copy files or build artifacts to a remote machine ...

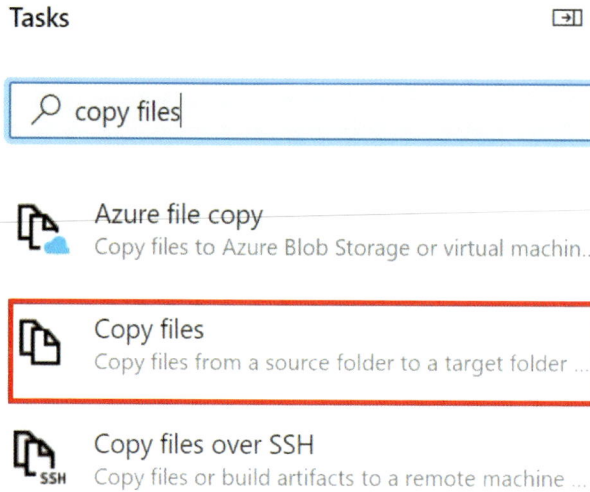

Figure 116: Copy files task

The source folder is optional. By default, it will use the root folder of your code repository. This can be accessed by the variable *$(Build.SourcesDirectory)*. Under Contents, specify the location to our dist folder, relative to the Source Folder. Type in **dist/**** to select all the content under the dist folder. Finally, specify the target folder by adding the variable *$(Build.ArtifactStagingDirectory)* to specify the artifact staging directory in Azure pipelines.

💡 Be aware that for Linux build agents you have to use "/" path separator when specifying paths.

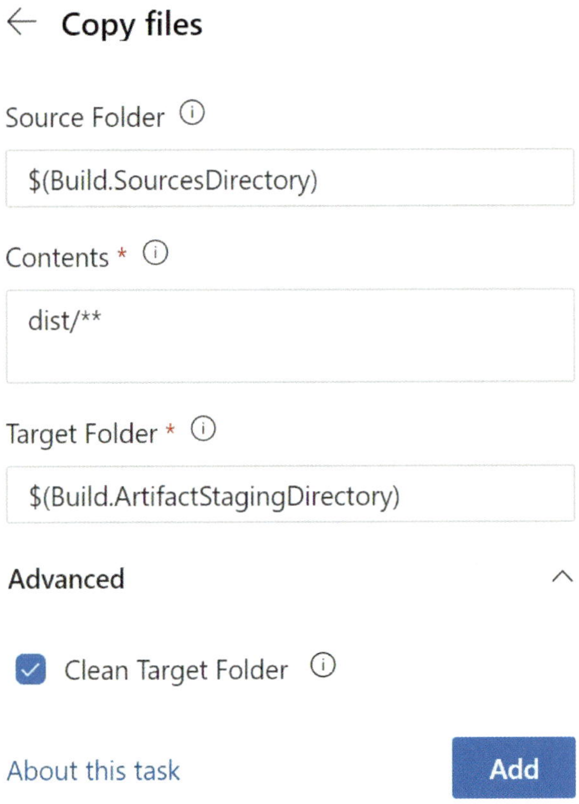

← **Copy files**

Source Folder ⓘ

$(Build.SourcesDirectory)

Contents * ⓘ

dist/**

Target Folder * ⓘ

$(Build.ArtifactStagingDirectory)

Advanced ⌃

✓ Clean Target Folder ⓘ

About this task   **Add**

Figure 117: Settings for copy files

Archive the copied files

Then archive the copied **dist** folder using a preferred compression format. So, click on the show assistant button on the right and search for **archive files** task and select it.

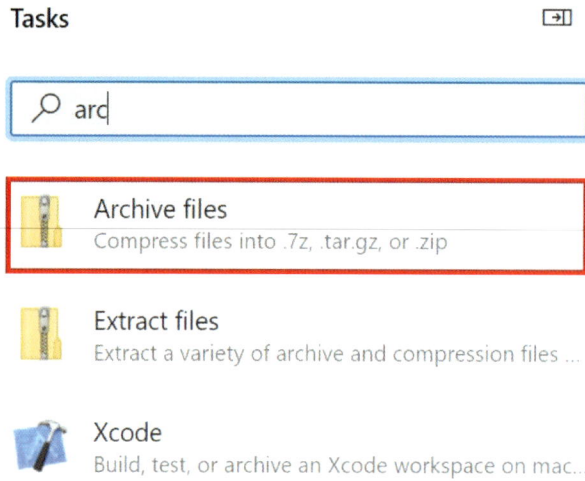

Figure 118: Archive files task

The options for this task are shown in Figure 119. The root folder is the dist folder copied to the artifact staging directory, and the drop.zip file will be created on the same artifact staging directory.

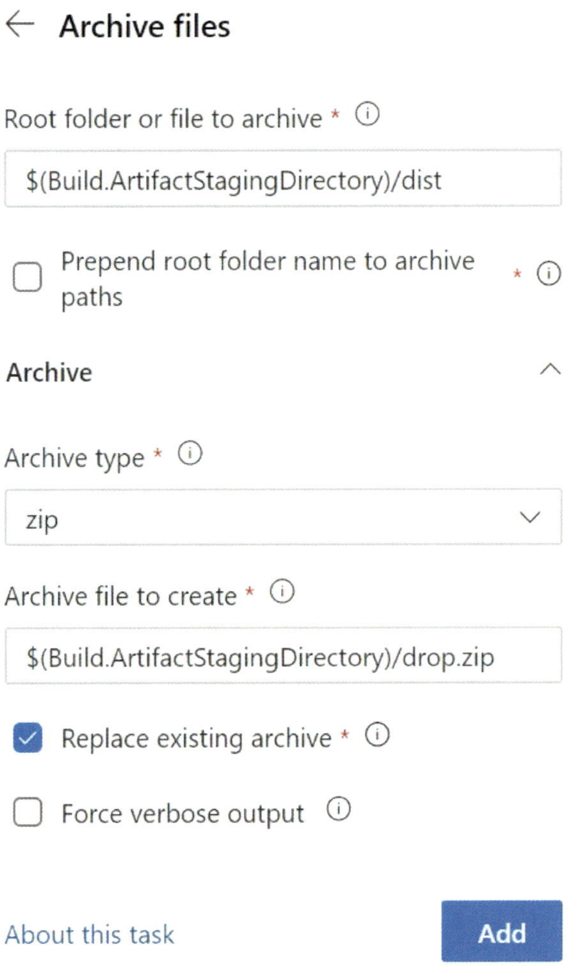

← **Archive files**

Root folder or file to archive * ⓘ

$(Build.ArtifactStagingDirectory)/dist

☐ Prepend root folder name to archive paths   * ⓘ

Archive   ∧

Archive type * ⓘ

zip   ∨

Archive file to create * ⓘ

$(Build.ArtifactStagingDirectory)/drop.zip

☑ Replace existing archive * ⓘ

☐ Force verbose output ⓘ

About this task   **Add**

Figure 119: Options for Archive files task

Publish artifact to Azure pipelines

In the third step, we need a **publish build artifacts** task. In the *Tasks window*, type "publish" to find the task **Publish build artifacts** and click to select it.

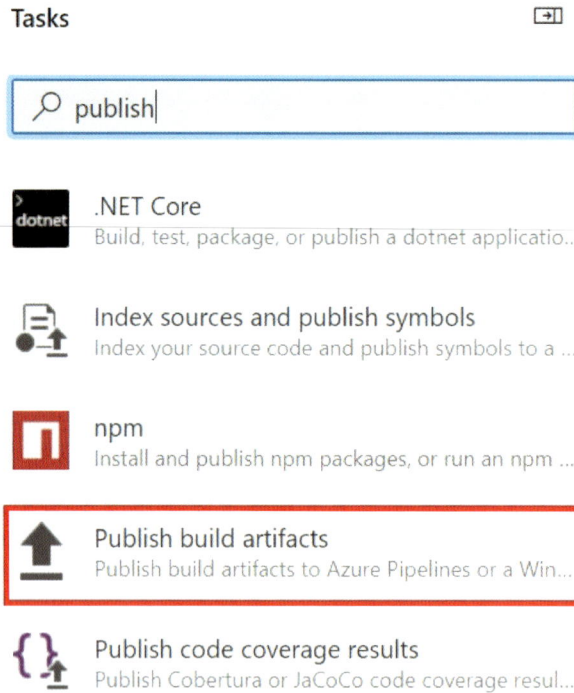

Figure 120: Publish build artifacts task

Now, we have 3 options to consider here. First, specify where your build output resides at the moment. As a result of the archive files task, our deployment ready files are located in *$(Build.ArtifactStagingDirectory)/drop.zip* folder. Next, you can provide a name to your artifact created in the first step. Finally, you specify where your artifact is going to be placed. This can be under your build agent - **Azure Pipelines** or in a file share which build agent can find. Here, we select the default Azure Pipelines and click **Add**.

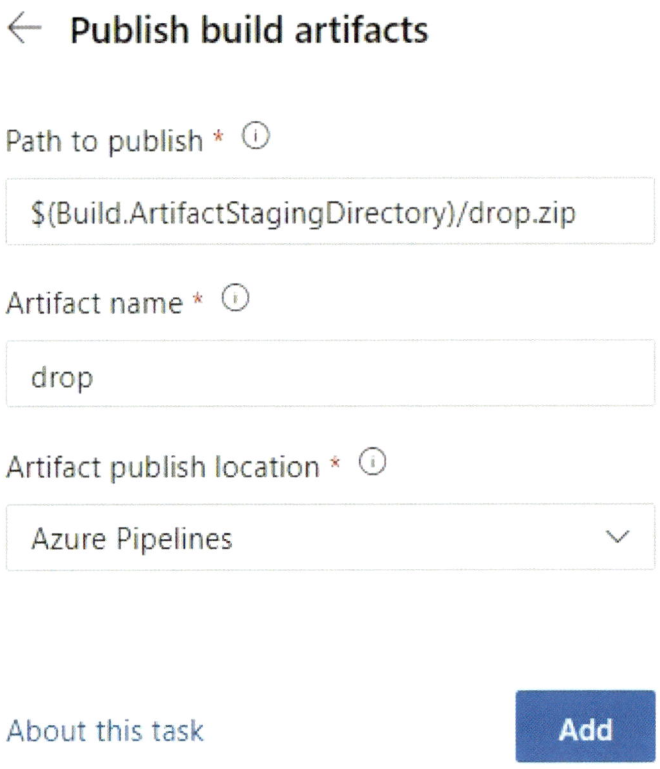

← **Publish build artifacts**

Path to publish * ⓘ

```
$(Build.ArtifactStagingDirectory)/drop.zip
```

Artifact name * ⓘ

```
drop
```

Artifact publish location * ⓘ

```
Azure Pipelines                              ⌄
```

About this task   **Add**

Figure 121: Inputs for Publish build artifacts task

All the steps in the yaml file are listed as follow.

```
steps:
Settings
- task: NodeTool@0
  inputs:
   versionSpec: '10.x'
  displayName: 'Install Node.js'

- script: |
    npm install
    npm run build
  displayName: 'npm install and build'

Settings
- task: CopyFiles@2
  inputs:
    SourceFolder: '$(Build.SourcesDirectory)'
    Contents: 'dist/**'
    TargetFolder: '$(Build.ArtifactStagingDirectory)'
    CleanTargetFolder: true

Settings
- task: ArchiveFiles@2
  inputs:
    rootFolderOrFile: '$(Build.ArtifactStagingDirectory)/dist'
    includeRootFolder: false
    archiveType: 'zip'
    archiveFile: '$(Build.ArtifactStagingDirectory)/drop.zip'
    replaceExistingArchive: true

Settings
- task: PublishBuildArtifacts@1
  inputs:
    PathtoPublish: '$(Build.ArtifactStagingDirectory)/drop.zip'
    ArtifactName: 'drop'
    publishLocation: 'Container'
```

Figure 122: Final build pipeline code

This is not the only way to publish your build artifacts to the staging area. So feel free to play around with different tasks to find out different ways to publish to the staging folder.

Save and run the build pipeline

Once you have finalized your build pipeline, it is now time to save all the changes. Click on the button **Save and run** to save the pipeline in your source code and run it immediately.

Variables | **Save and run** ∨

Now, you will be asked to save the azure-pipelines.yml file to your repository. Here, you can provide a message and commit either to the master branch or to a new branch. As we have setup a policy against committing directly to our master branch, we have to create a new branch for this and merge the changes to the master branch through a pull request.

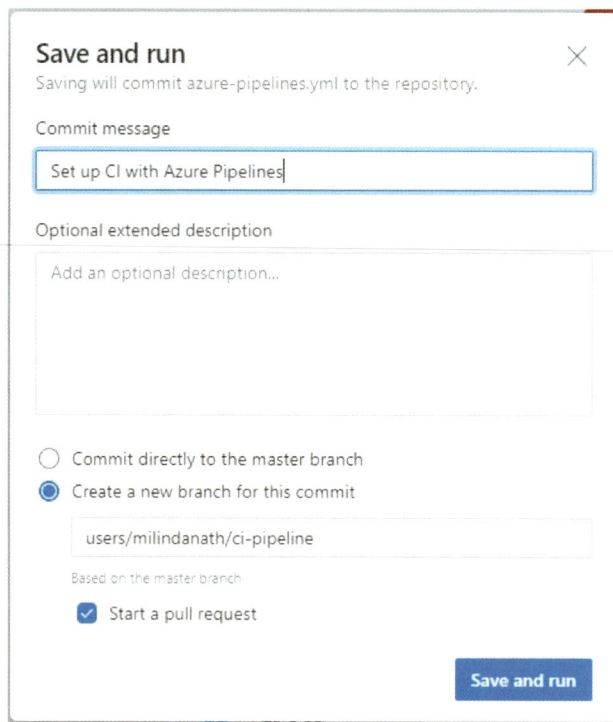

Figure 123: Pull request to merge the pipeline file

When your build pipeline runs, the build agent begins one or more jobs. In this case, we have only one job, and it starts under the section **Jobs** as shown in Figure 124. Click on **Job** to see the ongoing build process.

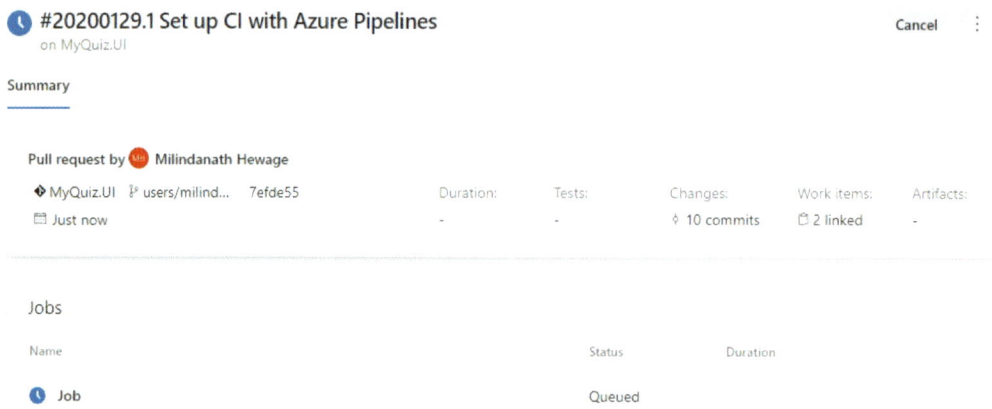

Figure 124: Build pipeline starting its jobs

Jobs in run #20200201.1
MyQuiz.UI

Jobs

Job — 38s

- Initialize job — 1s
- Checkout MyQuiz.UI@users/milin... — 1s
- Install Node.js — 2s
- npm install and build — 29s
- CopyFiles — 1s
- PublishBuildArtifacts — 1s
- Post-job: Checkout MyQuiz.UI@... — <1s
- Finalize Job — <1s
- Report build status — <1s

Job

```
1   Pool: Azure Pipelines
2   Image: ubuntu-latest
3   Agent: Hosted Agent
4   Started: Today at 1:21 PM
5   Duration: 38s
6
7 ▶ Job preparation parameters
8   🗂 1 artifact produced
```

Figure 125: Build pipeline summary after the run

After successful completion of the build pipeline, we end up with a deployable build artifact as shown in Figure 125. If you click on that, you can see which files will be deployed when you deploy your application.

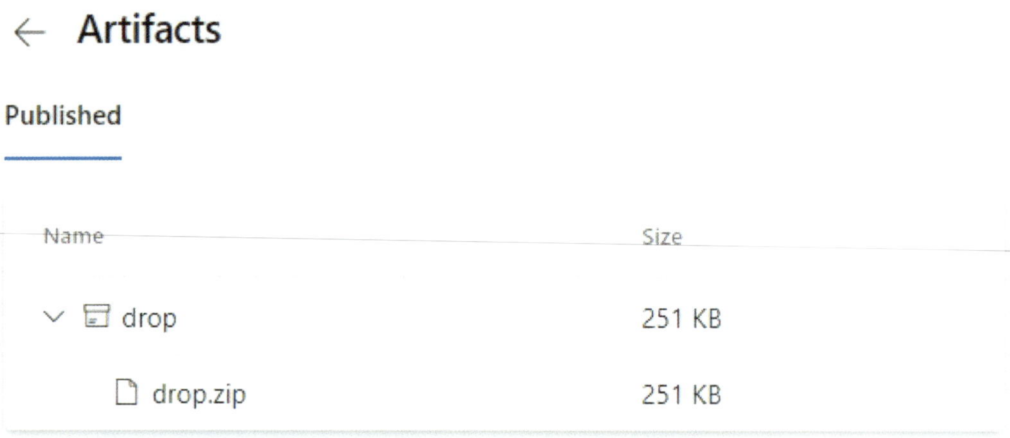

← **Artifacts**

Published

Name	Size
⌄ ▤ drop	251 KB
🗎 drop.zip	251 KB

Figure 126: Drop folder (Output of the build process)

Edit the build pipeline

If you click on the Pipelines menu on the left pane, you will see our new build pipeline as shown in Figure 127.

Recently run pipelines

Pipeline	Last run
✅ MyQuiz.UI	#20200201.1 • Merged PR 4: Cha... 🗓 2h ago
	⬦ Individual CI ⑂ master ⏱ 34s

Figure 127: Newly created build pipeline

You can edit this pipeline by clicking on MyQuiz.UI row and then by clicking on the **Edit** button.

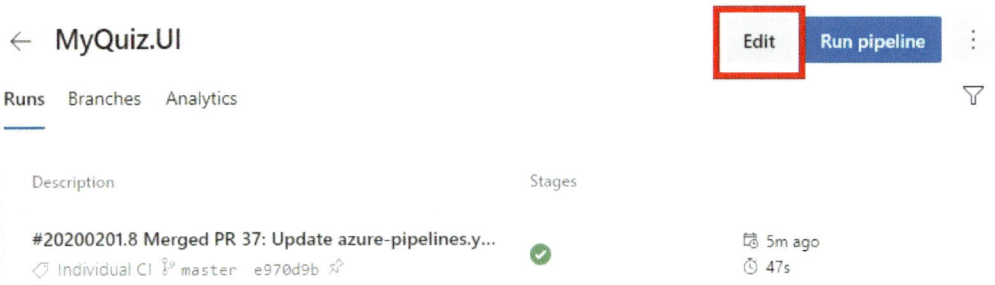

Figure 128: Edit pipeline

Build summary

You can click on the first item in the list to see the build summary. It shows the following information related to the build

1. *who triggered the build*
2. *code repository, branch and commit in which the build was run*
3. *date and time of the build*
4. *duration it took to run*
5. *how many commits involved in the build*
6. *how many work items linked*
7. *the produced artifact*

These are highlighted in the Figure 129.

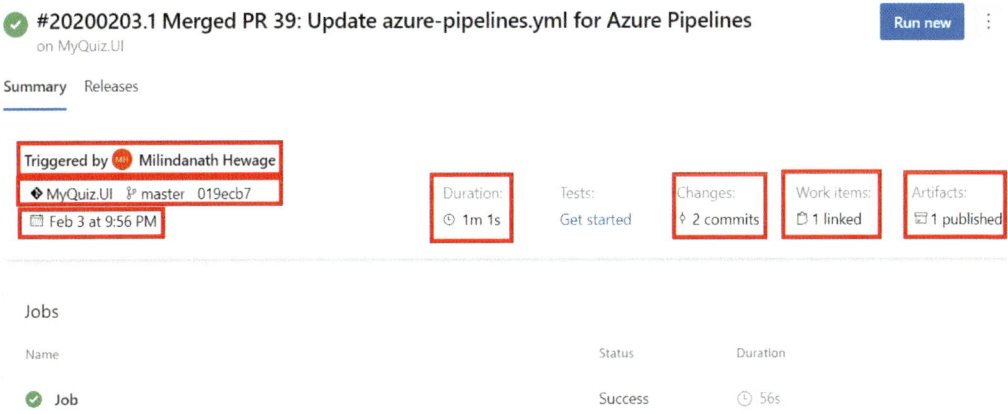

Figure 129: Build Summary

Approve pull request

If you examine your master branch, you will notice that the yaml configuration file for our build is not yet added to the master branch. It is waiting for the approval through the pull request created while saving our build pipeline. Once you approve the pull request, you can see that the yaml file will be part of your source code.

Having the build configuration file together with the source code is a very nice feature. This gives you the possibility to go back to previous versions of your source code at any given time and build the project without any problems using the configuration you used in that exact same version. In other words, you can version control your build pipeline.

Disable the pipeline

If you want to disable / pause the build pipeline, you can do it through the edit page. Click on the options button on the right and select **Settings**.

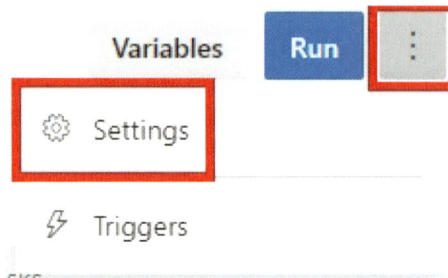

Inside the settings page, you can select either paused or disabled option to disable the build pipeline. Click on the **Save** button to save your changes.

Continuous Delivery (CD)

We have automated our build process using the build pipeline. So, the next step is to automate the deployment process using a release pipeline (CD pipeline). Before creating the release pipeline, you will have to design your release pipeline.

Release environment

In the example shown in Figure 130, we have 3 *stages/deployment phases* in the release pipeline. First a **Dev** environment where you deploy the build artifacts and perform initial testing. Then, you deploy it to the **Test** environment where your test team quality assures the application thorough testing before deploying to production. You can also have a staging environment between test and production (Although I have skipped in this example).

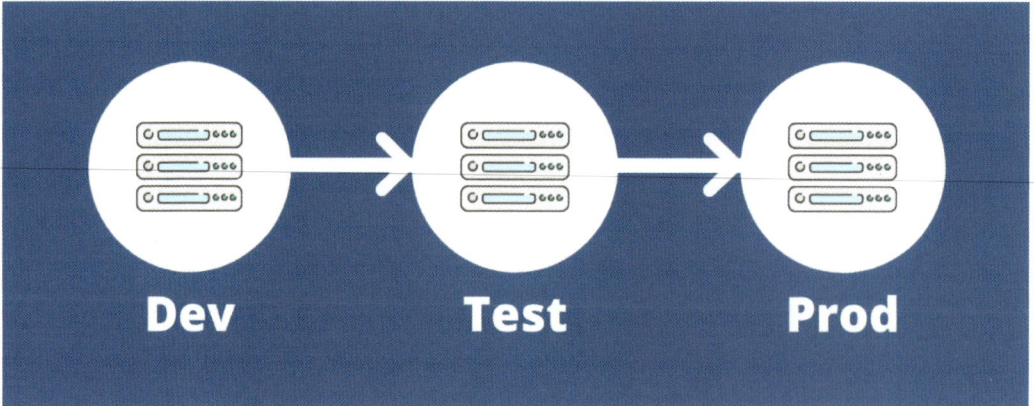

Figure 130: Deployment strategy

The release environments which are connected to these 3 stages can come in different forms based on your preference. It could be an IIS web app on an on-premise server/Virtual Machine, a containerized environment like Kubernetes, a managed service like Azure App service, or a serverless environment like Azure functions. Let us use Azure App service to deploy our application.

You can navigate to *https://azure.microsoft.com/en-us/* to access the Microsoft Azure web site. If you have not created an Azure account yet, you can create a new account for free.

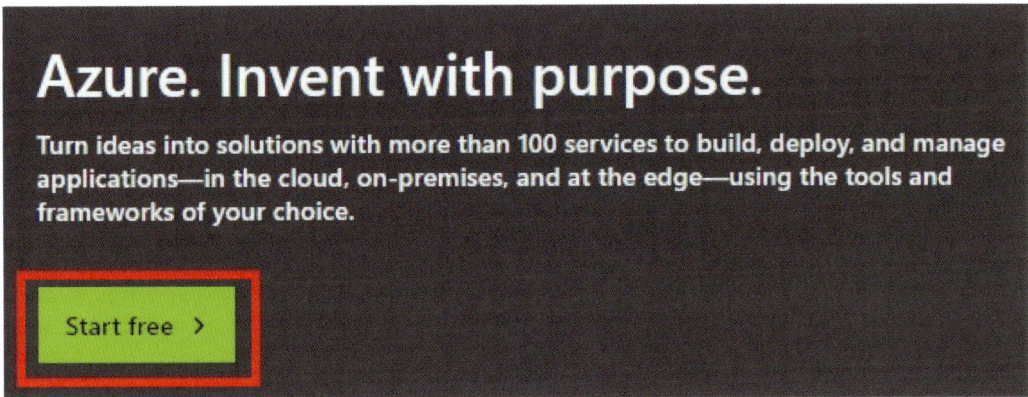

Azure. Invent with purpose.

Turn ideas into solutions with more than 100 services to build, deploy, and manage applications—in the cloud, on-premises, and at the edge—using the tools and frameworks of your choice.

Start free >

Figure 131: Azure front page

Once you are finished with the account creation, navigate to https://portal.azure.com/#home to access the Azure portal. Click on the **Create a resource** link on the home page.

Azure services

+
Create a resource

App Services

$ Cost Management...

Figure 132: Create a new resource in Azure

Now find out the **Web app** option from the next window and click on it.

Ubuntu Server 18.04 LTS

Learn more

Web App

Quickstart tutorial

Figure 133: Create a Web App Service

Follow these steps to complete the rest of the process.

1. Select your Azure subscription
2. Create a new resource group by clicking on the Create new link

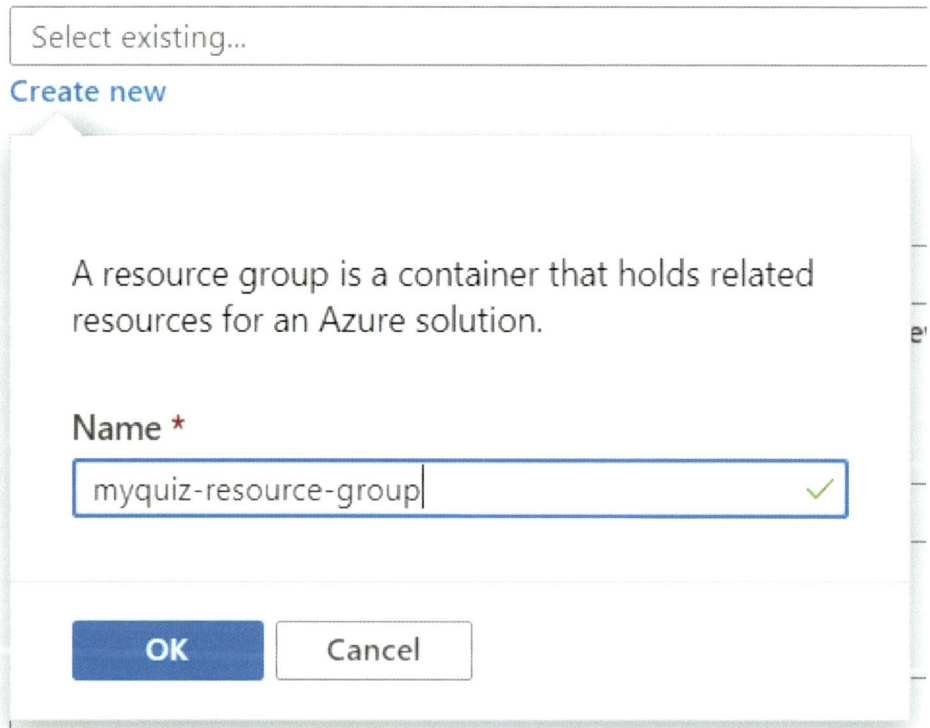

Select existing...

Create new

A resource group is a container that holds related resources for an Azure solution.

Name *

myquiz-resource-group

OK   Cancel

3. Next, provide a name for your web app for the Dev environment. Let us say we want to call our dev url *milindanath-myquiz-dev.azurewebsites.net*.

4. Then, select a runtime stack that matches the application. As we developed our application in node.js version 12, select Node 12 LTS.

Instance Details

| Name * | milindanath-myquiz-dev | ✓ |
| | | .azurewebsites.net |

Publish * (**Code** Docker Container)

Runtime stack * [Select a runtime stack. ∧]

Operating System * **Node**

Region * Node 12 LTS

Node 10 LTS

5. Now, select an operating system.
6. Then, select a region matching and close to your area.
7. Create an app service plan and **remember to select a Free F1 tier** if you want to start with a basic app for free. You can change the **Sku and size** by clicking on the **change size** link.

Windows Plan (North Europe) * ⓘ   (New) myquiz-app-service-plan

Create new

Sku and size *   **Standard S1**
100 total ACU, 1.75 GB memory
Change size

Spec Picker

Dev / Test

For less demanding workloads

- -

Recommended pricing tiers

F1

Shared infrastructure
1 GB memory
60 minutes/day compute
Free

8. After everything is filled in, click on the **Review + create** button to create the app service for your dev environment.

Sku and size *

Free F1
Shared infrastructure, 1 GB memory
Change size

| Review + create | < Previous | Next : Monitoring > |

Repeat the same process to create the other two environments - *test* and *production*. The final setup of the environment is as shown in Figure 134.

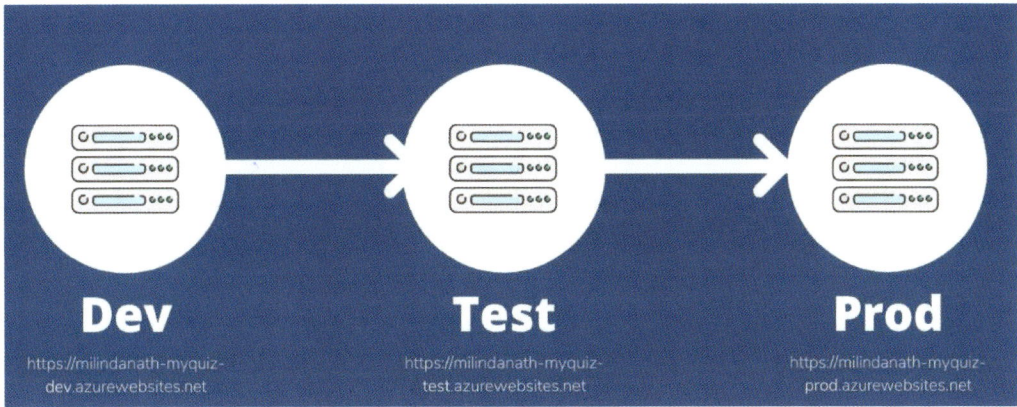

Figure 134: Release environments with Azure App Service URLs

Create the release pipeline

Click on Pipelines -> Releases to navigate to release pipeline page.

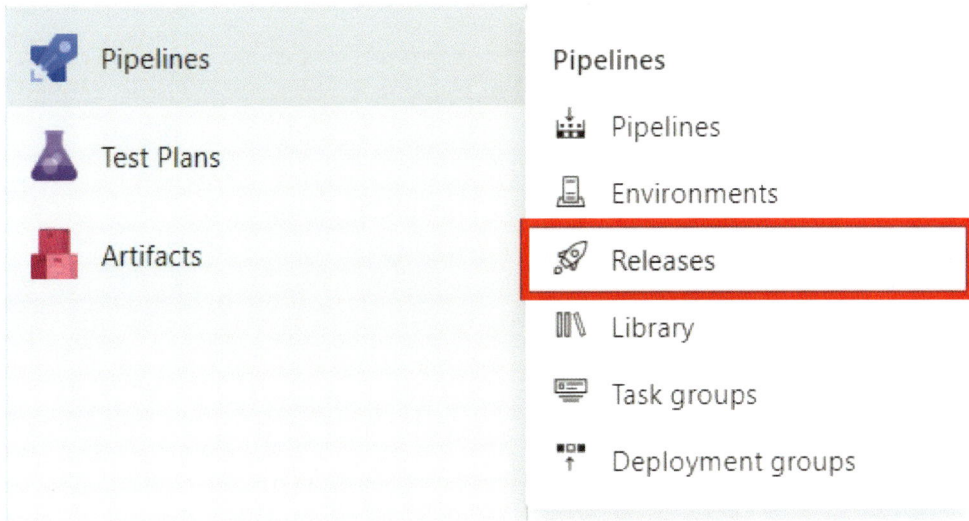

Figure 135: Releases menu item

Now click on the **New pipeline** button to create your first release pipeline.

No release pipelines found

Automate your release process in a few easy steps with a new pipeline

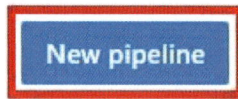

New pipeline

Figure 136: New pipeline button

As we want to deploy our application to Azure, select the option **Azure App Service deployment** and click on the **Apply** button as shown in Figure 137.

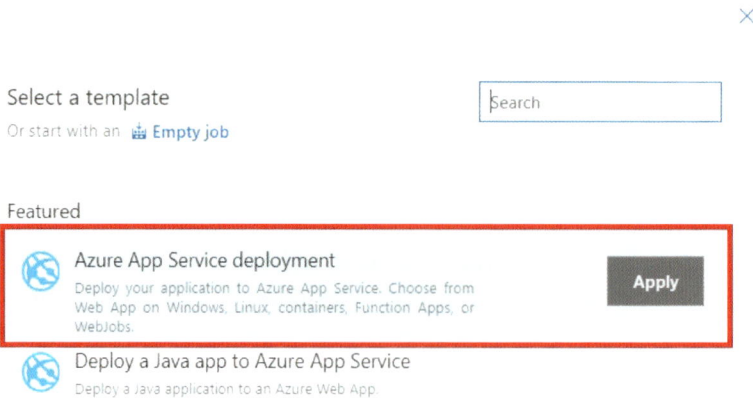

Select a template   Search
Or start with an 🏗 **Empty job**

Featured

Azure App Service deployment   Apply
Deploy your application to Azure App Service. Choose from
Web App on Windows, Linux, containers, Function Apps, or
WebJobs.

Deploy a Java app to Azure App Service
Deploy a Java application to an Azure Web App.

Figure 137: Azure App Service deployment template

In the next window, you have to specify to which stage you are going to deploy to. According to our plan, the first stage we want to deploy our code is **Dev**. Therefore, select **Dev** environment as shown in Figure 138.

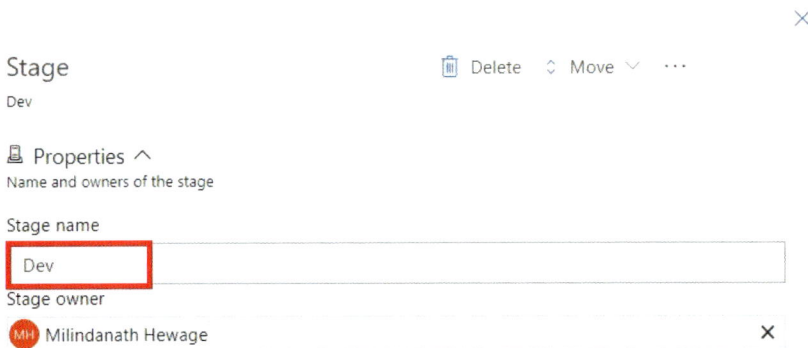

Figure 138: Dev stage

Once you close this dialog, you can see that the Dev stage is created. Each stage has one or more jobs that runs on a release agent. You can navigate to the stage configuration page by clicking on one of the highlighted links in Figure 139.

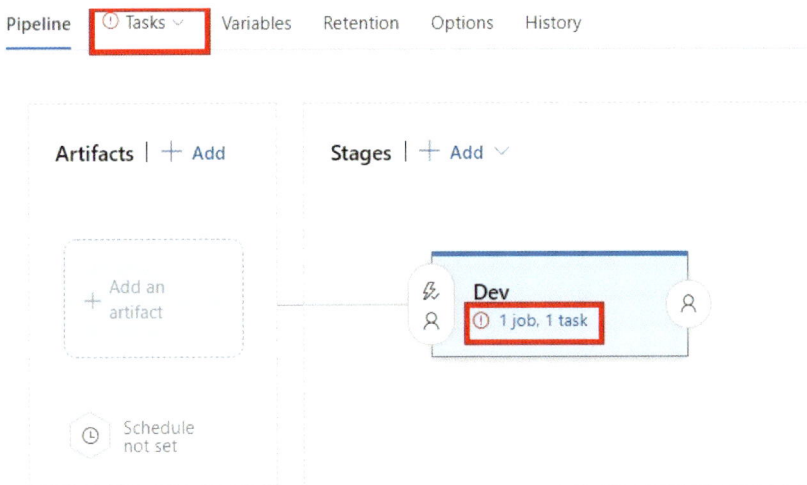

Figure 139: Navigate to stage configuration

First, click on the **Dev** to setup the basic stage settings.

Here, you have to specify 2 mandatory fields. The first one is your **azure subscription**. If nothing is shown in the dropdown, click on the **Manage link** to connect your azure subscription to Azure DevOps. In the second option, select the **App service name** which was created when setting up the release environments.

Now we have successfully connected our Azure App Service Dev environment to the Dev stage in the pipeline. Now, click on the **Run on agent** section to select an agent from the **Azure Pipelines** agent pool. Let us keep the default configuration for this and move on to the task **Deploy Azure App Service**.

However, before moving even further with the Dev stage setup, we have to provide the **artifact** we created in the build pipeline as an input to the release pipeline. Click on the **Pipeline tab** and then click on add link or on the **Add an artifact** links to add this as shown in Figure 140 and Figure 141.

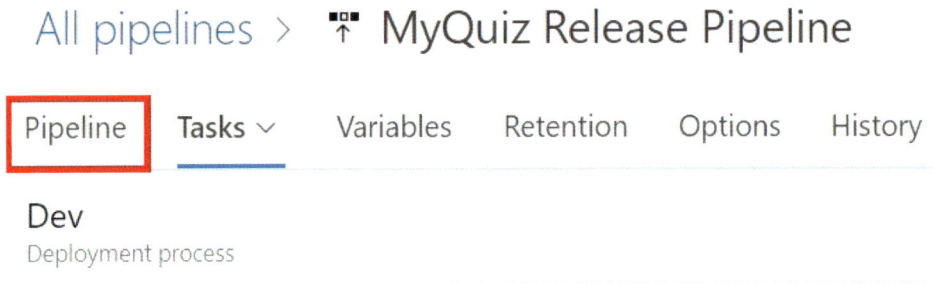

All pipelines >   MyQuiz Release Pipeline

| Pipeline | Tasks ∨ | Variables | Retention | Options | History |

Dev
Deployment process

Figure 140: Pipeline tab

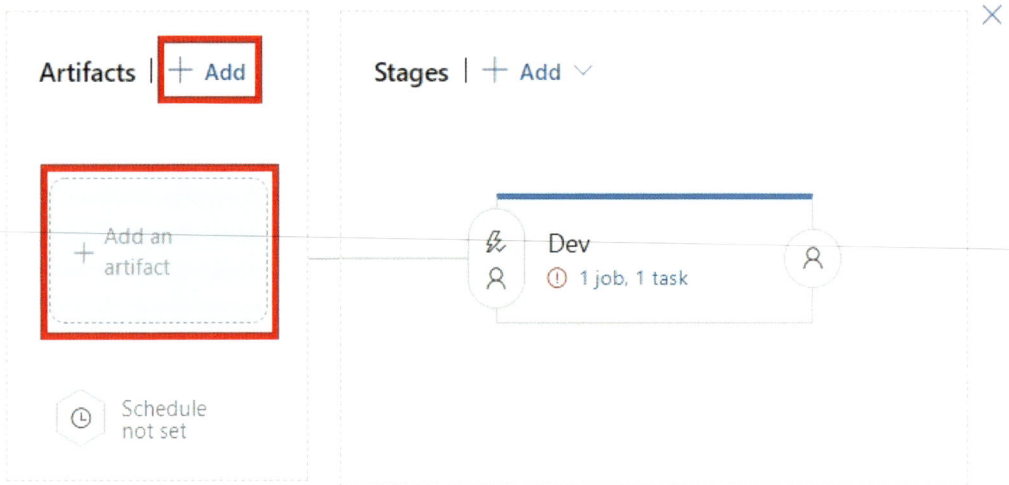

Figure 141: Add an artifact links

In **add an artifact** window, Select **Build** as the Source type. Then, select your project and the build pipeline name as shown in Figure 142. You can also specify which version of the artifact should be used when the release pipeline runs. Here, we take the **latest** version of the artifact.

✕

Add an artifact

Source type

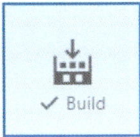

5 more artifact types ∨

Project *   ⓘ

PracticalGuide   ∨

Source (build pipeline) *   ⓘ

MyQuiz.UI   ∨

Default version *   ⓘ

Latest   ∨

Source alias *   ⓘ

MyQuiz_Dist

ⓘ The artifacts published by each version will be available for deployment in release pipelines. The
    latest successful build of **MyQuiz.UI** published the following artifacts: ***drop***.

Add

Figure 142: Add an artifact window

Click on the **Add** button to add the artifact as the input to the release
pipeline.

Trigger release pipeline

One of the key features in DevOps automation is continuously deliver
your product to the customers. In order to do that, we have to enable
continuous integration for your release pipeline. We can do it in two ways
as discussed below.

Method 1: By scheduling a new release at a specific time

In this page, you have the possibility to run your release pipeline on a regular basis. For example, suppose you want to run your release every **Tuesday at 03:00 a.m** whenever there is a new build available. In that case, you can click on the button **Schedule** as shown in Figure 143.

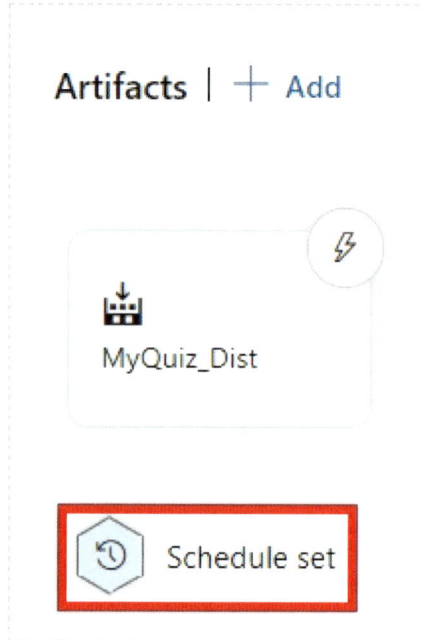

Figure 143: Schedule set button

In the next window, enable *Create a new release at the specified times* option, and set the times as shown in Figure 144.

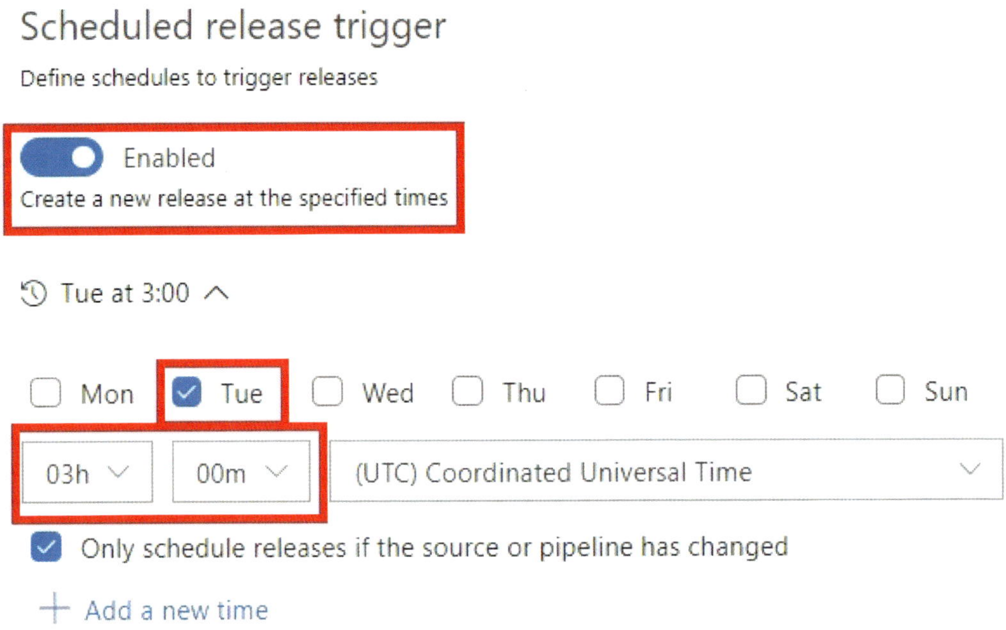

Scheduled release trigger

Define schedules to trigger releases

Enabled
Create a new release at the specified times

🕑 Tue at 3:00 ⌃

| ☐ Mon | ☑ Tue | ☐ Wed | ☐ Thu | ☐ Fri | ☐ Sat | ☐ Sun |

| 03h ⌄ | 00m ⌄ | (UTC) Coordinated Universal Time ⌄ |

☑ Only schedule releases if the source or pipeline has changed

+ Add a new time

Figure 144: Trigger releases on every Tuesday 3 o'clock

Method 2: Each time a new build is available

The other method is to trigger the release, each time the build pipeline produces a new artifact. If you revisit the build pipeline, it will produce an artifact each time you commit changes to the master branch. Click on the button **Continuous deployment trigger** button as shown in Figure 145.

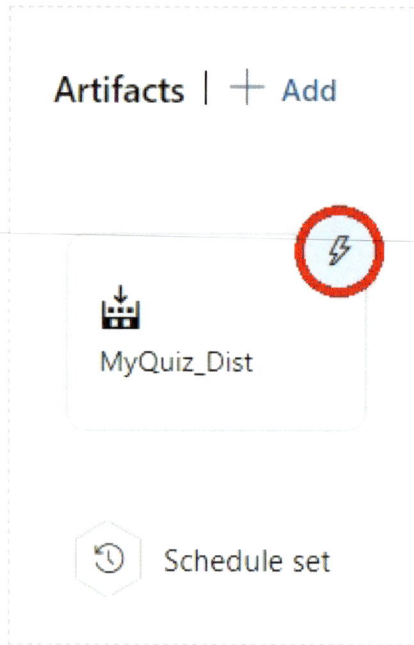

Figure 145: Continuous deployment trigger button

Enable the **Continuous deployment trigger** option to enable this feature. By default, this will select the master branch to trigger this event.

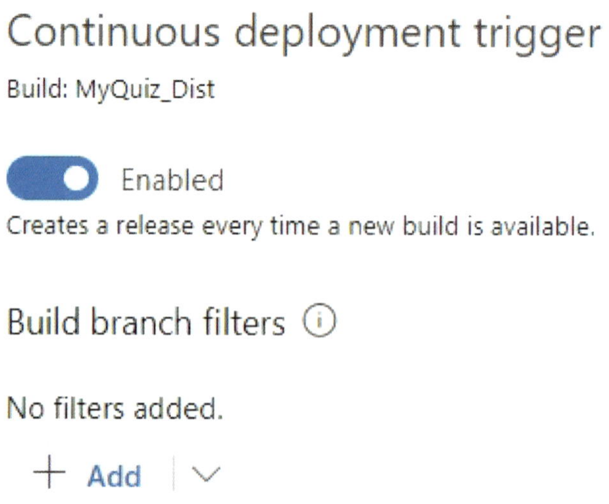

Figure 146: Continuous deployment trigger for master branch

Suppose you do not want to trigger a release for the master branch build, but for another branch, then you can use the **Build branch filters** option. For example, if you want to trigger a release each time you create a branch under the **releases** folder, then you can do it as shown in Figure 147.

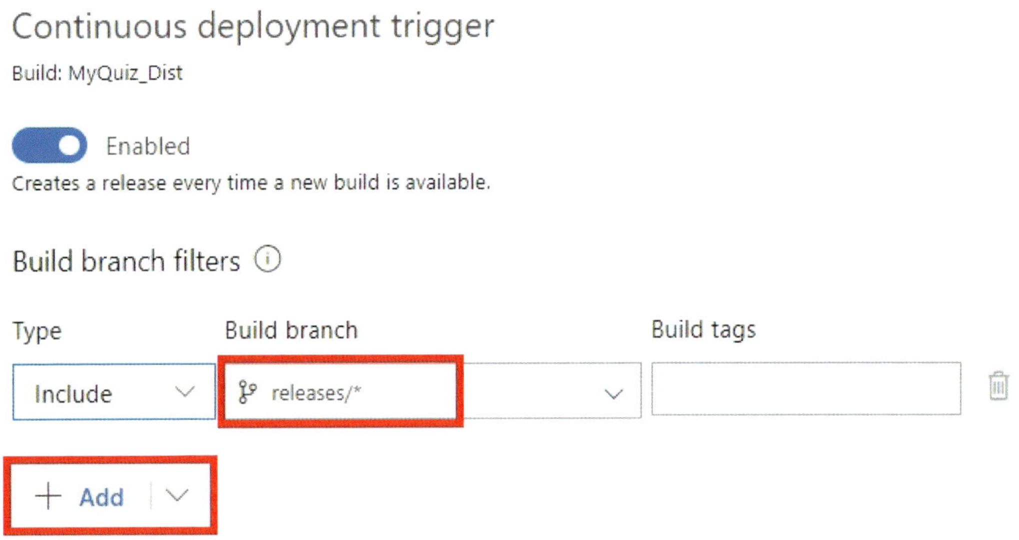

Figure 147: Trigger release for builds in releases folder

Finalize the Azure app service task

Now, we can go back to our tasks list, and finalize the Deploy to azure app service task. So, click on the Tasks menu, and then click on the Deploy to Azure App Service task. What is important here is to provide the path to your drop.zip file.

Scoped to subscription 'Pay-As-You-Go'

App Service type *

Web App on Windows

App Service name *

milindanath-myquiz-dev

☐ Deploy to Slot or App Service Environment ⓘ

Virtual application ⓘ

Package or folder * ⓘ

$(System.DefaultWorkingDirectory)/MyQuiz.Dist/drop/drop.zip   ...

Figure 148: Azure app service deployment task options

Rename the build pipeline

Now, we have setup our release pipeline. Before saving, let us rename our pipeline to a suitable name. I am going to call it *MyQuiz Release Pipeline*. To do that, click on the current name which is shown on the breadcrumb on the top.

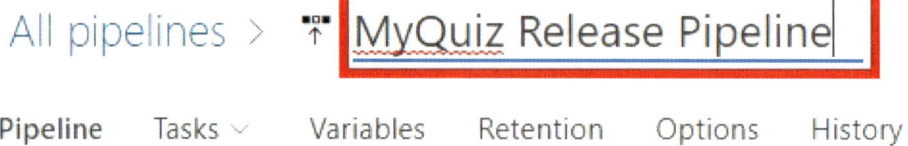

All pipelines > ⵜ MyQuiz Release Pipeline

Pipeline   Tasks ⌄   Variables   Retention   Options   History

Figure 149: Rename the release pipeline

Release options and variables

In Azure pipelines, you can make use of variables to contain variable data that can be used in different places. There are pre-defined variables defined by Azure DevOps. For example, the variables we used earlier such as *$(Build.SourcesDirectory)* are pre-defined variables. Moreover, you can create your own custom variables.

Click on the **Variables** tab in your release pipeline to create some custom variables.

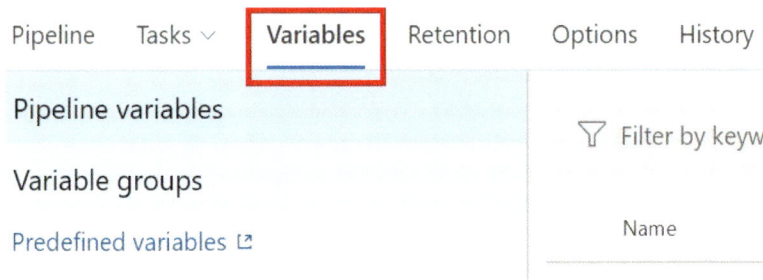

Figure 150: Variables tab

Click on the **Add** button to create variables to represent the major and minor versions of the release.

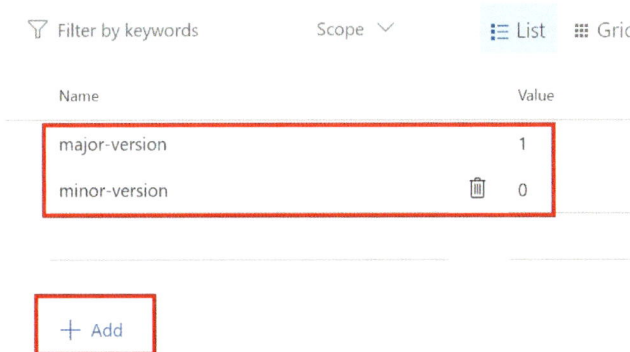

Figure 151: Set major and minor versions using variables

Now we can change the format of the release name using these custom variables. You can set additional information such as the format of the release name under the tab **Options**. Here, we combine the two custom variables with the pre-defined variable *$(Build.BuildNumber)* to create a unique name for the release.

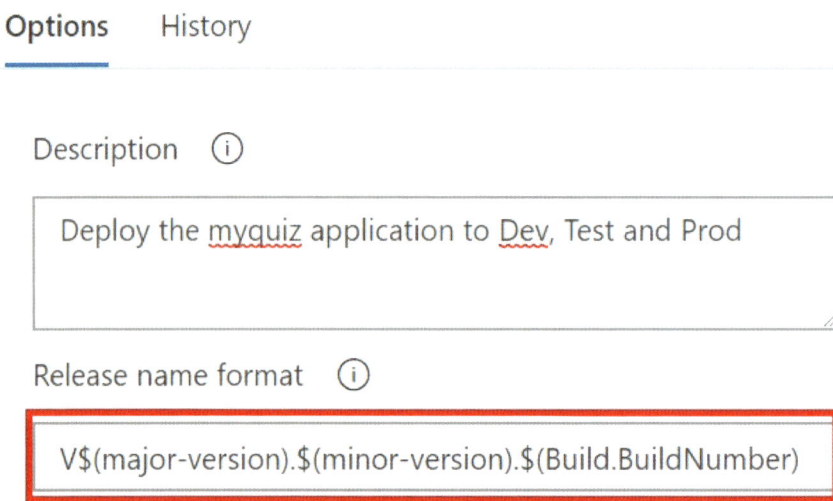

Figure 152: Change the release format name using variables

Now click on the **Save** button to save all the changes done to the pipeline.

Edit release pipeline

You can edit your pipeline by navigating to the **Releases** section from the **Pipelines** navigation pane. Now select the newly created pipeline and click on the Edit button.

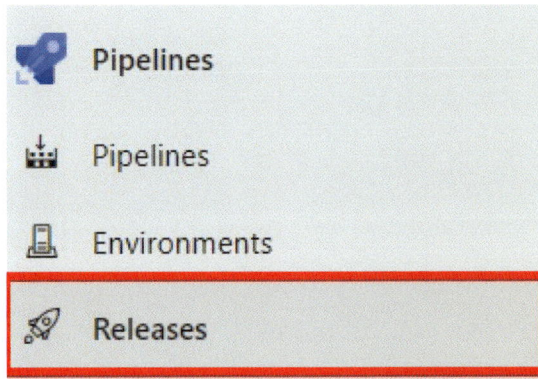

Figure 153: Pipelines -> Releases

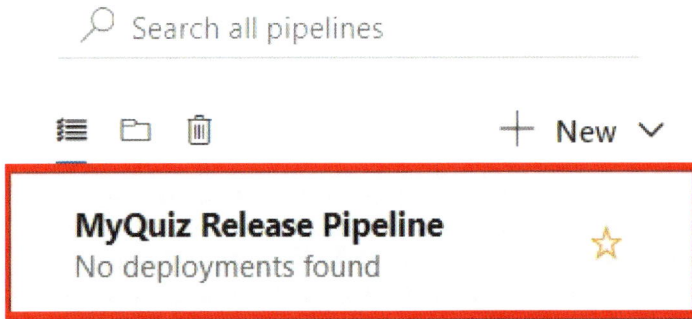

Figure 154: New release pipeline

End to end testing of the pipelines

As we have finalized setting up both the build and release pipelines, let us try to do a full end to end test to check that the whole process we defined so far works as expected.

Create a new task

Suppose, one of the testers in our team finds out that our home page has the Vue.js logo. So, he creates a task to fix this issue.

📗 **1** Create a GUI for the application	✅ **6** Create a color palette that can be used throughout the site
EM Eric Martin **16 h**	**EM** Eric Martin **5**
State ● To Do	State ● To Do
Priority 2	Priority 2

✅ **15** Remove the Vue logo from the home page

MH Milindanath He...

State ● To Do

Priority 2

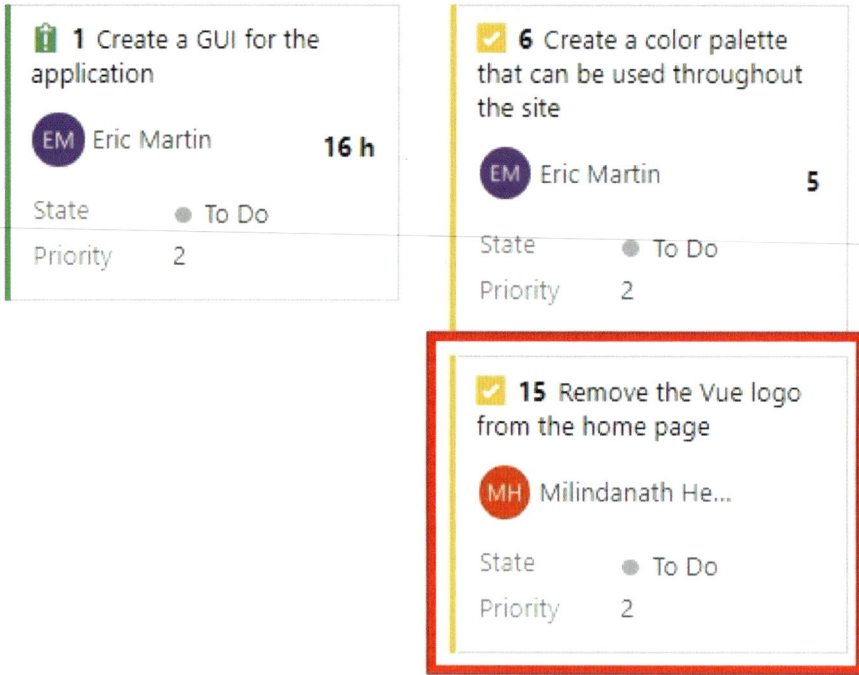

Figure 155: New work item reporting the issue

Create a new branch for the task

The next step is to create a new branch for the task. Let us do it in VS Code terminal using the following git command.

```
$ git checkout -b bug/15
```

Fix the bug

Navigate to the views folder and open Home.vue file and remove the img tag to fix the issue.

```
<template>
  <div class="home">
    <img alt="Vue logo" src="../assets/logo.png">
    <HelloWorld msg="Welcome to Your Vue.js App"/>
  </div>
</template>
```

Figure 156: Fix the issue by removing the img tag

Commit and push changes

Commit and push your changes to the remote repository.

$ git add src/views/Home.vue

$ git commit -m "#15 Removed the Vue logo"

$ git push origin bug/15

Create the pull request

Now, go back to your Azure DevOps services and click on Azure Repos. You will see the option to Create a pull request. Click on the button.

Contents   History

ⓘ   You updated ⅄ bug/15 Just now   Create a pull request   ✕

Figure 157: Create a new pull request

Next, approve your changes to accept the changes and merge them into the master branch.

Build pipeline kicks off

Remember that we have setup our build pipeline so that every commit to the master branch will trigger the build pipeline. Let us find out if it kicks off the build. This can be seen in Figure 158.

Figure 158: Build pipeline starting

Release pipeline kicks off next

After the build pipeline succeeded, you will see that our release pipeline kicks off, and publish the application to Azure App Service. If everything has gone well, we get a green status on the Dev stage as shown in Figure 159

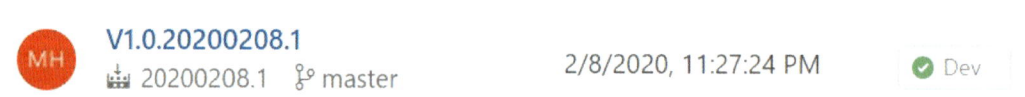

Figure 159: Successful deployment to Dev stage.

Click on the **Dev** button to inspect what has happened during the Deployment process. In this example, the release agent downloaded the artifact and published it to the Azure App service which is located at https://milindanath-myquiz-dev.azurewebsites.net/#/.

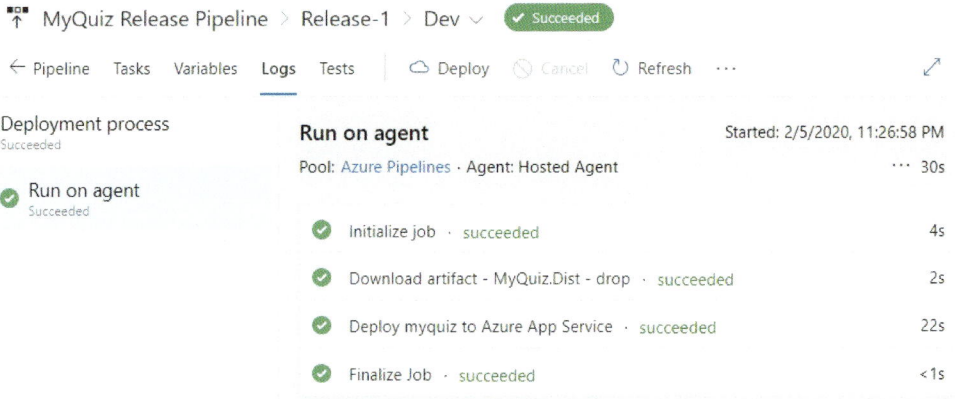

This can be verified by navigating to the dev URL located at https://milindanath-myquiz-dev.azurewebsites.net/#/ . You can see that the bug #15 is fixed and deployed.

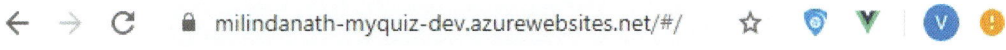

Figure 160: The deployment successfully published the change to the site

Congratulations! Now you have implemented end-to-end automation to your **Dev environment** using Azure Boards, Repos and pipelines.

Combine the pipelines

Probably you have noticed that there is an issue with our release pipeline. In the build pipeline, we created a *.yaml* file that defines the build process in code. That file is committed to the source control and get versioned with the build. Unfortunately, we do not have that facility in the release pipeline yet.

However, there is a method to write the release pipeline in yaml. It is by incorporating the release process into the build pipeline. Let us try to do that.

Extract the yaml code from the release pipeline

Navigate to your release pipeline and click on the Edit button. Now go to the Dev stage to view the tasks. Click on the **Deploy myquiz to Azure App Service** task. Now click on the link **View YAML**.

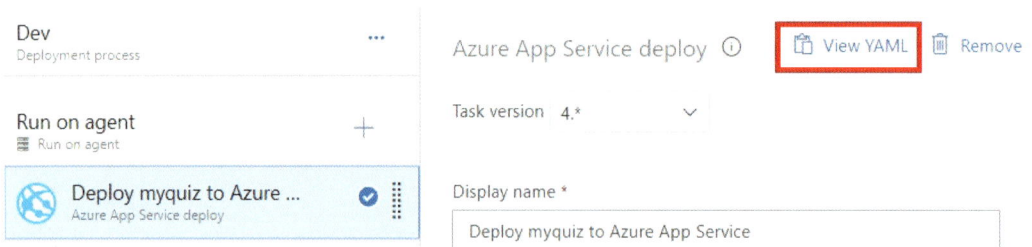

Figure 161: View the YAML code

Here, you can copy the web deployment step to clipboard. Click on the **Copy to clipboard** button.

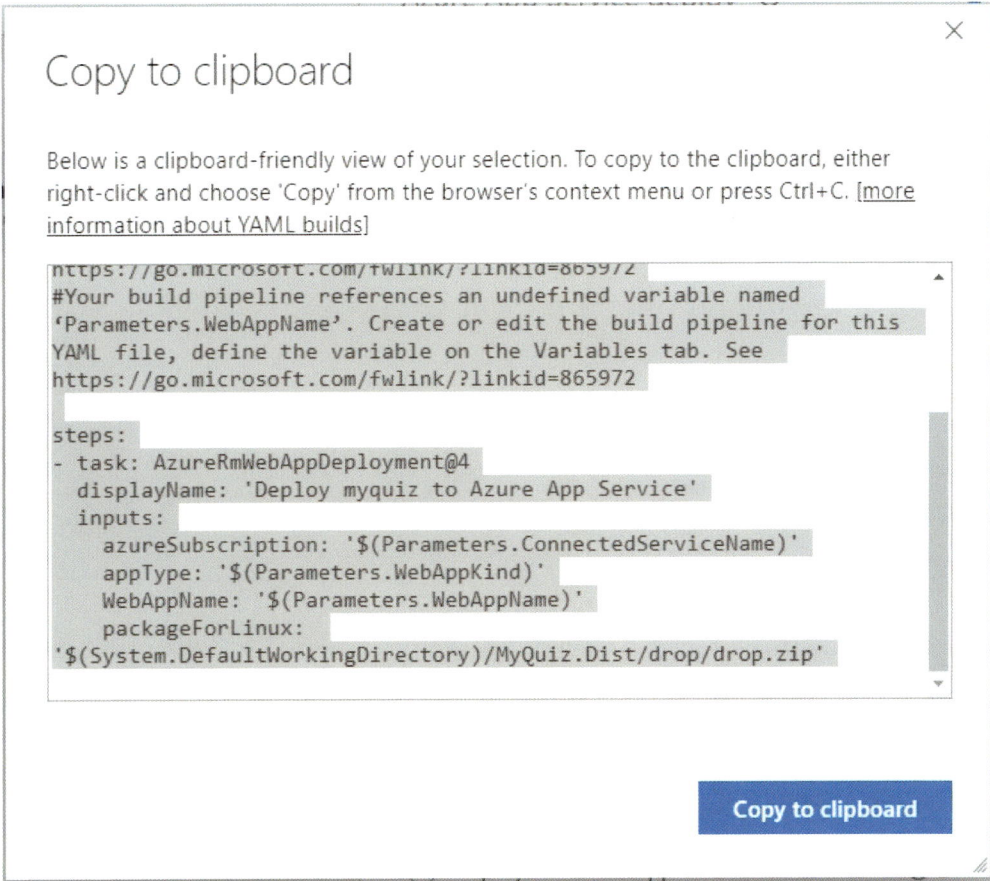

Figure 162: Copy the task to the clipboard

There are basically 3 variables you have to note down here.

1. $(Parameters.ConnectedServiceName), which is your azure subscription name
2. $(Parameters.WebAppKind) = webApp
3. $(Parameters.WebAppName) = milindanath-myquiz-dev

WebAppKind variable can have different values based on the deployment environment. Here are some of the options available.

1. webApp (used in this example)
2. webAppLinux

3. webAppContainer
4. functionApp
5. functionAppLinux
6. functionAppContainer

Add the yaml code to the build pipeline

First, open your build pipeline definition. Before pasting the yaml code copied to the clipboard, you have to add another task that downloads the zip files from the *artifact staging directory* to the *artifacts directory*. So, search for the **Download build artifacts** task as shown in Figure 163.

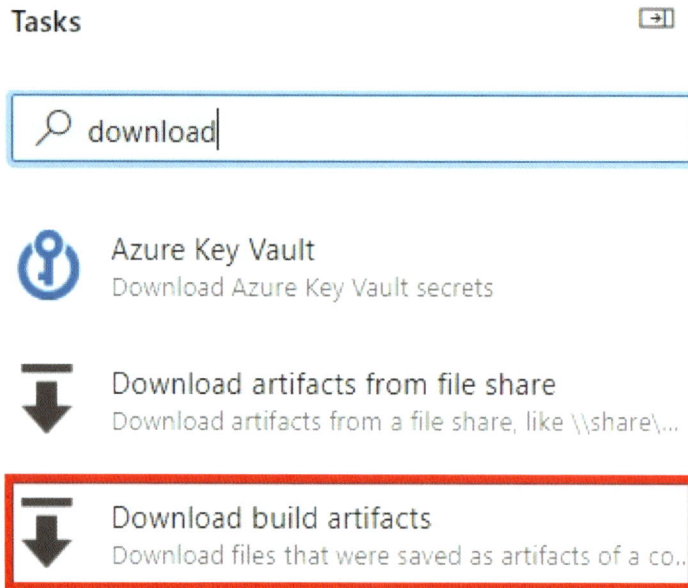

Tasks   ⇥

🔍 download

Azure Key Vault
Download Azure Key Vault secrets

Download artifacts from file share
Download artifacts from a file share, like \\share\...

Download build artifacts
Download files that were saved as artifacts of a co...

Figure 163: Search for download build artifacts task

Here, we download the drop artifact from the Artifact staging directory to the Artifact directory.

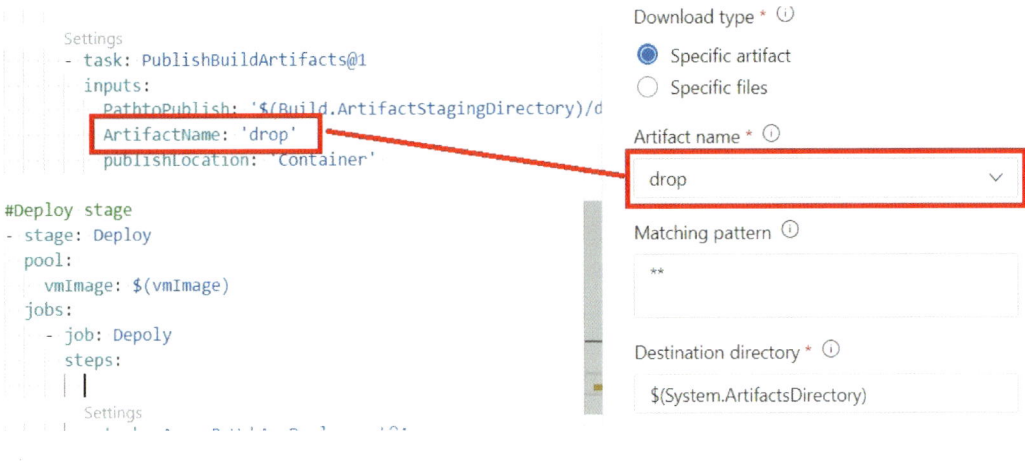

The final pipeline definition are as follows. The highlighted text are the new changes added to the previous build pipeline definition.

```
# Node.js with Vue
# Build and deploy a Node.js project that uses Vue.
# Add steps that analyze code, save build artifacts, deploy, and mor
e:
# https://docs.microsoft.com/azure/devops/pipelines/languages/javasc
ript

trigger:
- master

variables:
  Parameters.ConnectedServiceName: <<your_azure_subscription>>
  Parameters.WebAppKind: webApp
  Parameters.WebAppName: milindanath-myquiz-dev
  vmImage: 'ubuntu-latest'

stages:
  #Build stage
  - stage: Build
    pool:
      vmImage: $(vmImage)
      demands:
      - npm
    jobs:
```

```yaml
- job: Build
  steps:
  - task: NodeTool@0
    inputs:
      versionSpec: '10.x'
    displayName: 'Install Node.js'

  - script: |
      npm install
      npm run build
    displayName: 'npm install and build'

  - task: CopyFiles@2
    inputs:
      SourceFolder: '$(Build.SourcesDirectory)'
      Contents: 'dist/**'
      TargetFolder: '$(Build.ArtifactStagingDirectory)'
      CleanTargetFolder: true

  - task: ArchiveFiles@2
    inputs:
      rootFolderOrFile: '$(Build.ArtifactStagingDirectory)/dist'
      includeRootFolder: false
      archiveType: 'zip'
      archiveFile: '$(Build.ArtifactStagingDirectory)/drop.zip'
      replaceExistingArchive: true

  - task: PublishBuildArtifacts@1
    inputs:
      PathtoPublish: '$(Build.ArtifactStagingDirectory)/drop.zip'
      ArtifactName: 'drop'
      publishLocation: 'Container'

#Deploy stage
- stage: Deploy
  pool:
    vmImage: $(vmImage)
  jobs:
    - job: Depoly
      steps:
      - task: DownloadBuildArtifacts@0
        inputs:
```

```
buildType: 'current'
downloadType: 'single'
artifactName: 'drop'
downloadPath: '$(System.ArtifactsDirectory)'

- task: AzureRmWebAppDeployment@4
  displayName: 'Deploy myquiz to Azure App Service'
  inputs:
    azureSubscription: '$(Parameters.ConnectedServiceName)'
    appType: '$(Parameters.WebAppKind)'
    WebAppName: '$(Parameters.WebAppName)'
    packageForLinux: '$(System.ArtifactsDirectory)/**/*.zip'
```

Click on **save** and create a pull request. Before you approve the pull request, go to the release pipeline and disable the *continuous deployment trigger* and the *scheduled time* we add earlier. If you accept the pull request, you can see your code is built and deployed from one single pipeline file as shown in Figure 164. Most importantly, it will be committed to your source code.

When the build is starting it shows a progress icon as shown in Figure 164.

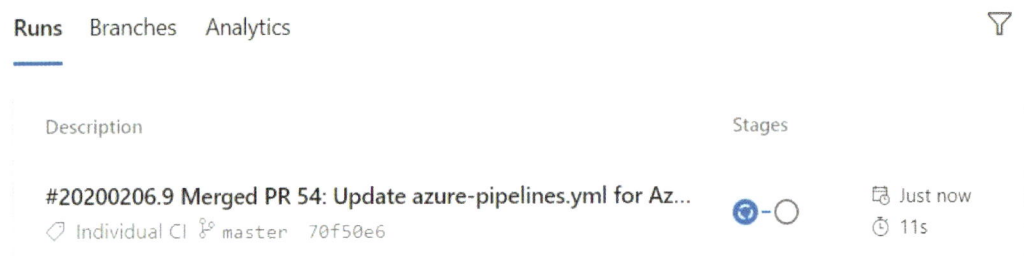

Runs Branches Analytics   ▽

Description	Stages	
#20200206.9 Merged PR 54: Update azure-pipelines.yml for Az... ◇ Individual CI ⑆ master 70f50e6	●–○	🖧 Just now ⏱ 11s

Figure 164: Multi-stage pipeline starting

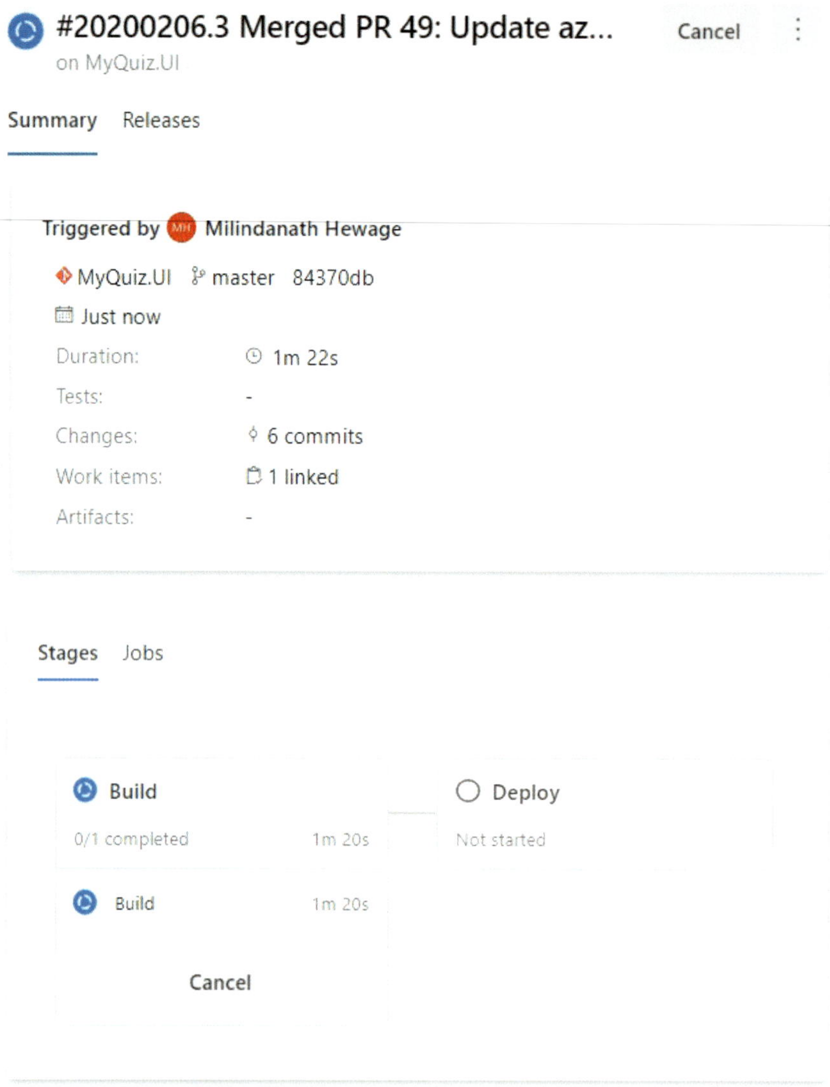

Figure 165: Release summary page

If you have not authorized your azure subscription, then you have to give permission to continue to deploy to azure as shown in Figure 166 and Figure 167.

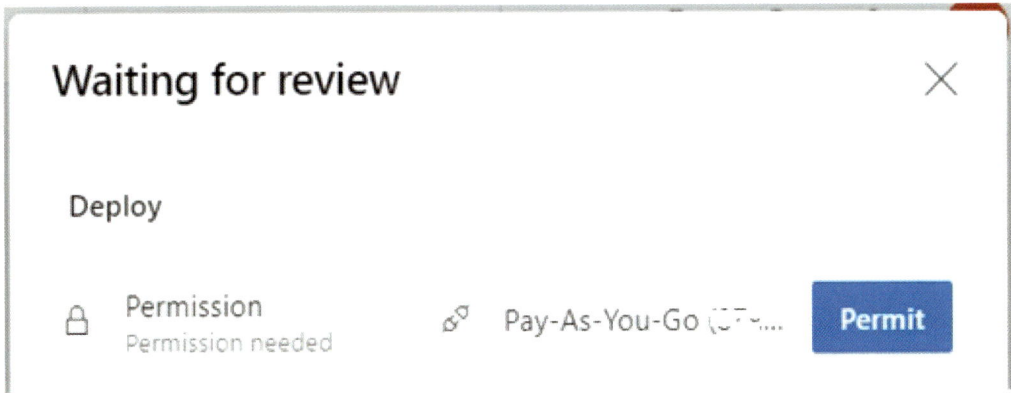

Figure 166: Give permission to access Azure subscription

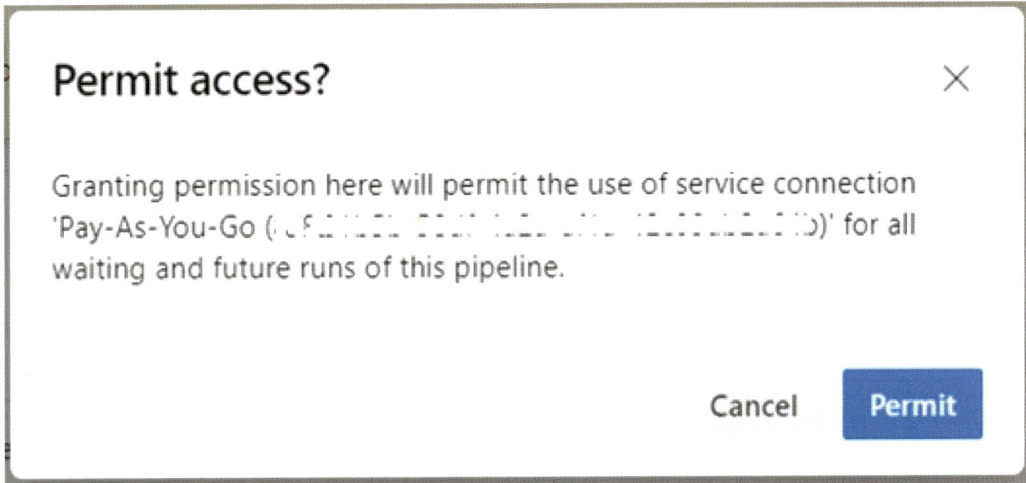

Figure 167: Grant permission

If the build and deploy stages are successful, you will see green status icons as shown in Figure 168.

Stages   Jobs

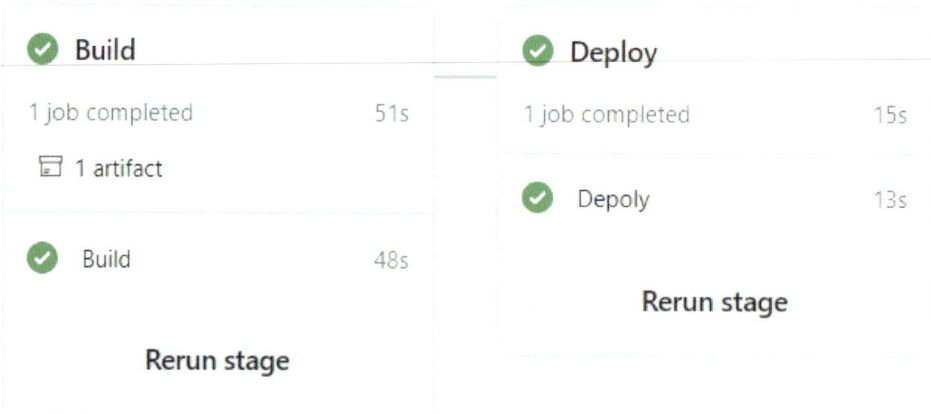

Figure 168: Successful runs of Build and Deploy stages

Test and Production environments

So far, we have only setup our Dev environment which is basically used by developers to test their changes in a build environment. However, when we do a full release of the application, we need to deploy it to a **test/QA** server where the testers can do their testing routines. However, we do not want that each developer's commit to the master branch gets deployed to the test or production environment.

Plan the release process

Suppose our team uses the trunk-based branching flow when dealing with the source code and releases. As we already have done, we create a branch when we want to try a new feature or a bug fix. Then we merge it to master branch using a pull request with code review.

We can use the same strategy when we want to do a release. Simply, create a branch off of master branch for the release and name the branch as release/1.0.

> Before moving into setting up the Test and Prod environments, remember to comment out the Deploy stage of your current build pipeline.

Let us change the build pipeline so that it triggers our build on any commit to any branch. However, we want to control the release pipeline.

```
6    trigger:
7    - '*'
```

Test stage

Go to the edit page of the release pipeline and clone the Dev stage.

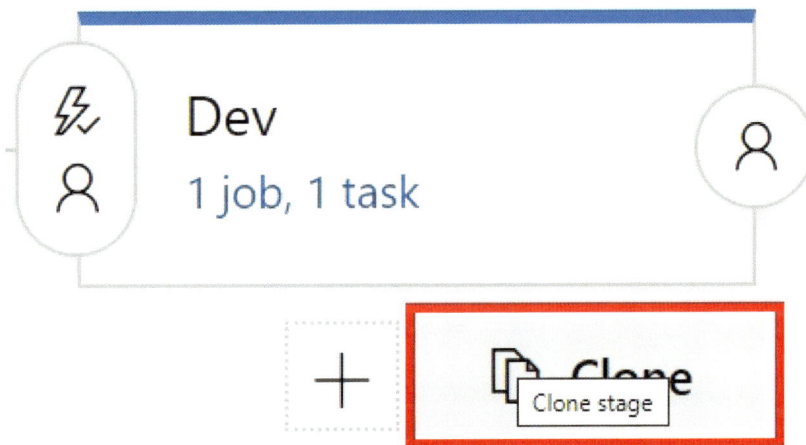

Figure 169: Clone the Dev stage

Rename the stage to **Test**.

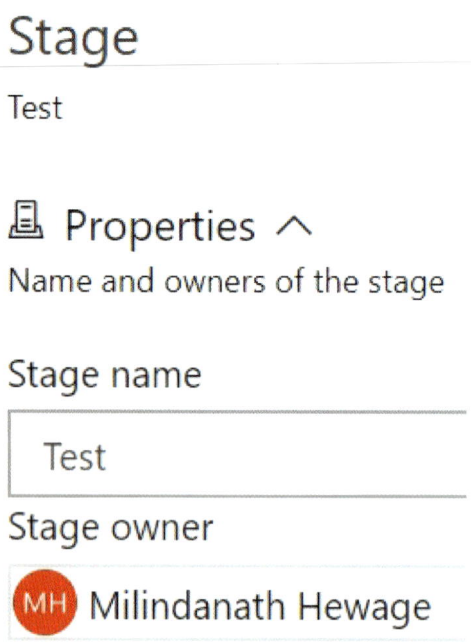

Stage

Test

🖳 Properties ^

Name and owners of the stage

Stage name

| Test |

Stage owner

(MH) Milindanath Hewage

Figure 170: Test stage

In the Tasks page, point the **App service name** to the correct azure test environment you created earlier.

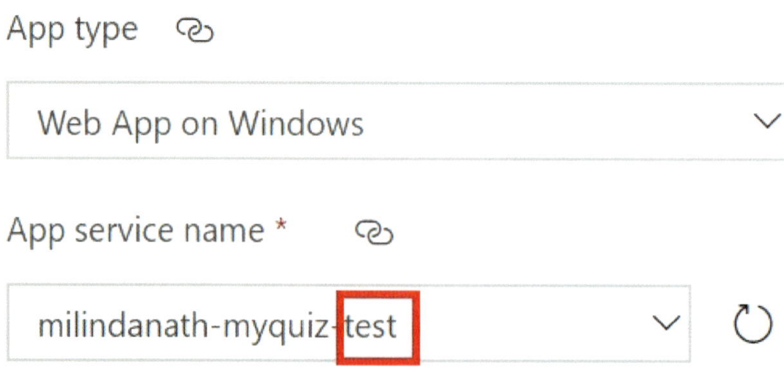

App type ᧖

| Web App on Windows   ∨ |

App service name *   ᧖

| milindanath-myquiz-test   ∨ | ↻

Figure 171: Set the correct app service name

Now, go back to the Pipeline tab, and click on the **pre-deployment conditions** button on the Test stage.

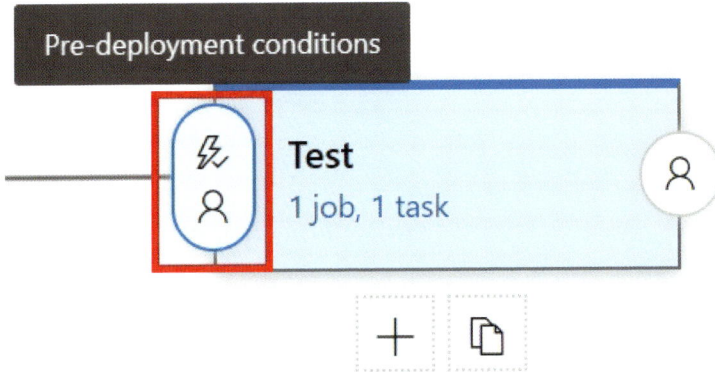

Figure 172: Pre-deployment conditions for the test stage

Select **After release** options under the **Triggers** section.

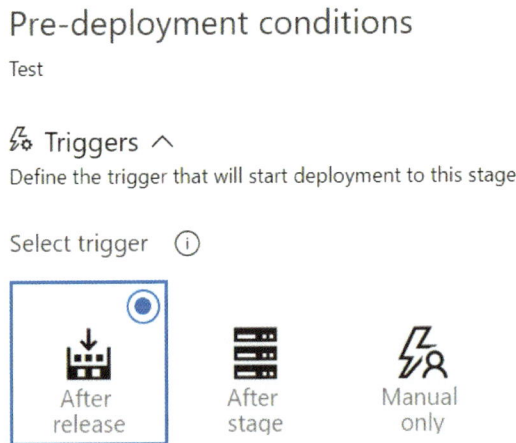

Figure 173: Select After release option

Now, enable Artifact filter and click on the Add button. Select the Artifact MyQuiz.Dist.

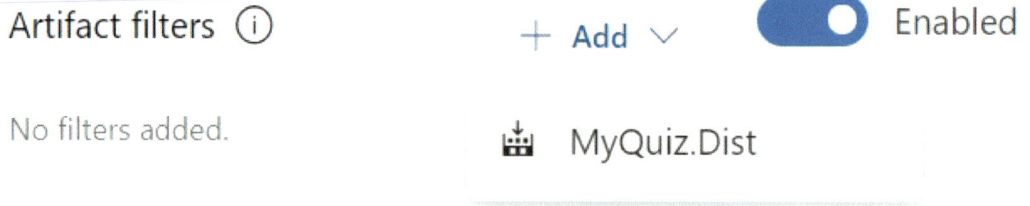

Artifact filters ⓘ   + Add ⌄   ⬤ Enabled

No filters added.   ⬇ MyQuiz.Dist

Figure 174: Artifact filters

Type in **releases/*** and press the enter key on the keyboard.

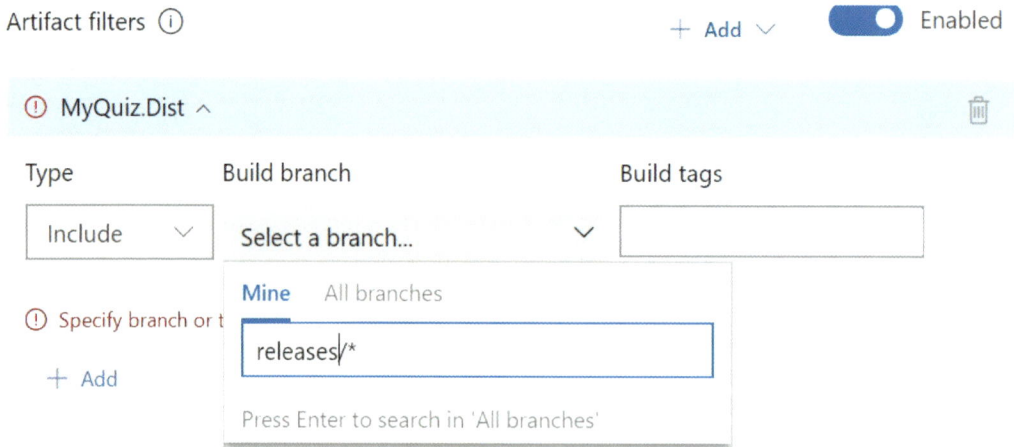

Artifact filters ⓘ   + Add ⌄   ⬤ Enabled

ⓘ MyQuiz.Dist ⌃   🗑

Type   Build branch   Build tags

Include ⌄   Select a branch...   ⌄   [   ]

                  Mine   All branches
ⓘ Specify branch or t
                  [releases/*   ]
  + Add
                  Press Enter to search in 'All branches'

Figure 175: Select releases branch

Close the window by clicking on the X button. Now you will see two stages are in parallel.

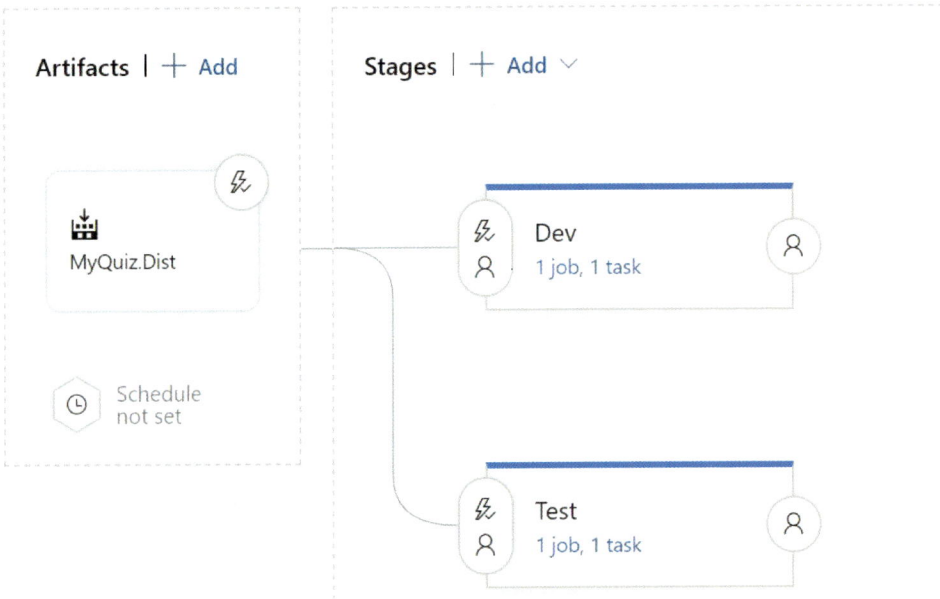

Figure 176: Dev and Test stages in parallel

However, the Test stage will only run when you create a branch under the path **releases/** . Dev stage will be triggered as usual for all the changes in any branch including the release branch.

Save everything and create a new branch off master branch. Create a pull request and merge it to master branch. In both cases, you will see that only Dev release will occur as shown in Figure 177.

Figure 177: Only dev stage is triggered

Now, let us create a new branch from the master and name it **releases/6**. After you create the branch, the build pipeline will kick off immediately.

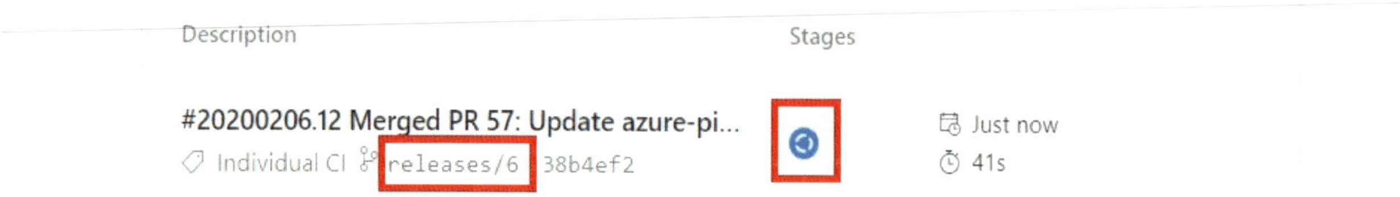

Figure 178: Build pipeline is starting

Not only that, it will deploy to both **Dev** and **Test** after the build is succeeded.

Figure 179: Both Dev and Test stages run

milindanath-myquiz-test.azurewebsites.net/#/

Home | About

Hello world, Welcome to MyQuiz

Question 1: Who is the founder of Microsoft?

- A: Bill Gates
- B: Satya Nadella
- C: Steve Jobs
- D: Mark Zuckerberg

Figure 180: myquiz test site

Production stage

The testing process is done, and it is time to deploy to production. So, we need to create a new stage for the prod environment. Clone the Test stage and rename it to Prod. Set the App service name to your production azure app service (here it is *milindanath-myquiz-prod*). Now the stages look like the following.

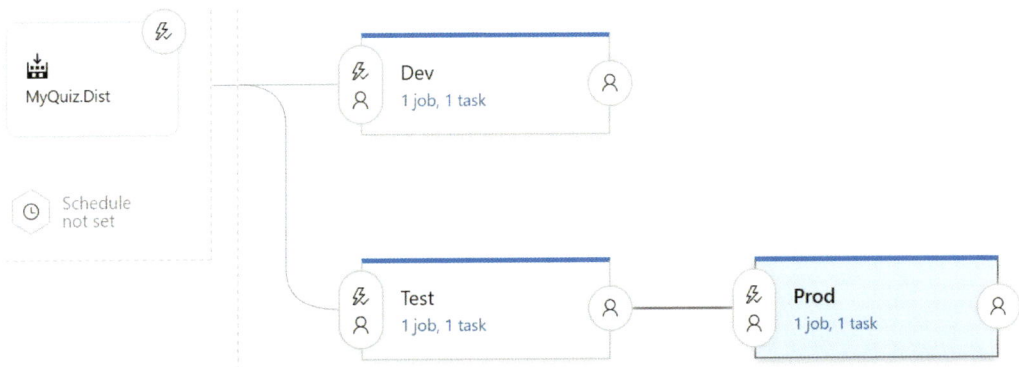

Figure 181: Prod stage is created

However, there is a problem with this setup. With this setup, the application will be deployed to both test and production each time you create a release branch. We do not want that to happen. So, we need some control here.

Approvals

This can be achieved by having approvals at certain key stages in the pipeline. For example, suppose your test team performs testing in the Test environment. Once they are satisfied with the testing, the leader of the test team or whoever responsible for testing, can approve the release to go forward. Let us see how we can achieve this.

Click on the **post-deployment conditions** button for the Test stage as shown in Figure 182

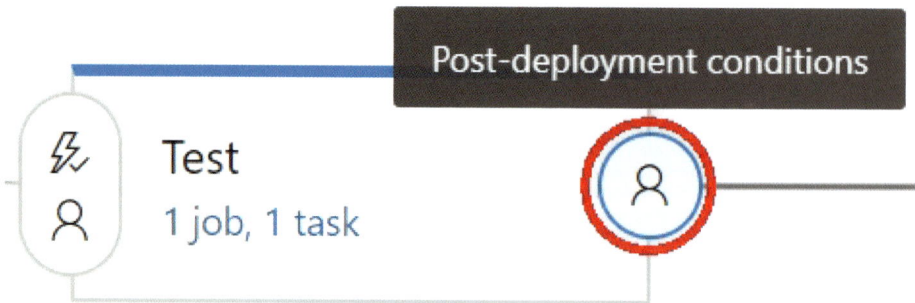

Figure 182: post-deployment conditions of the Test stage

Now enable post deployment approvals and select the test leader as the approver. Here, you can also setup approval policies as shown in Figure 183.

Post-deployment approvals ∧   ⬤ Enabled

Select the users who can approve or reject deployments to this stage

Approvers ⓘ

Test responsible

VE Viveka Edirisinghe ✕

Search users and groups for approvers

Timeout ⓘ

| 30 | Days ∨ |

Approval policies

☐ The user requesting a release or deployment should not approve it

☐ Revalidate identity of approver before completing the approval. ⓘ

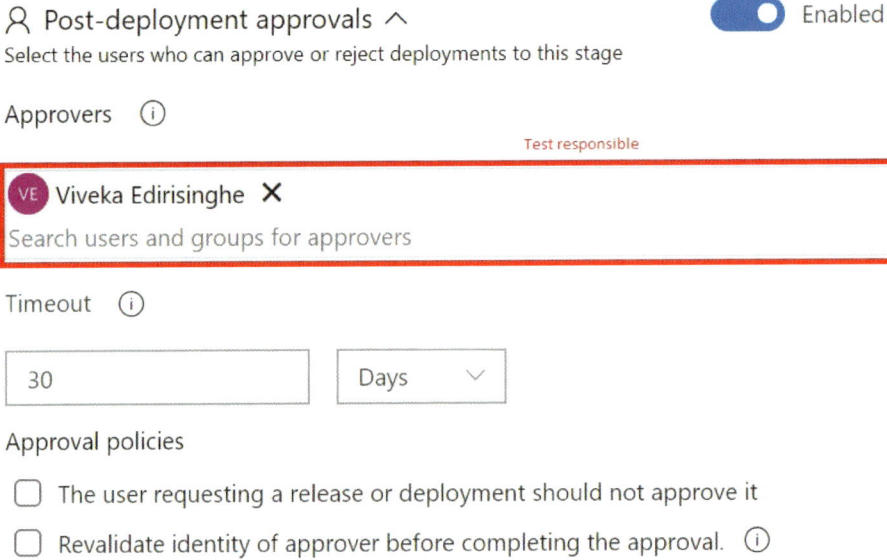

Figure 183: Select approver

Based on this, the release pipeline is paused at the Test stage until the test leader gives her permission to release to the production. Now, we have some control over the production release. But this control along might not be enough to release to the production. Probably, you need to perform some actions prior to every production release. For an example, your **Database Administrator (DBA)** wants to run the release scripts and other checks prior to production. We can setup the pre-deployment conditions of the Prod stage to achieve this.

Pre-deployment conditions

⚡
👤

Prod
1 job, 1 task

👤

Figure 184: pre-deployment conditions of Prod

Here you can assign your DBA as the approver, and without his clear signal the release will not go forward.

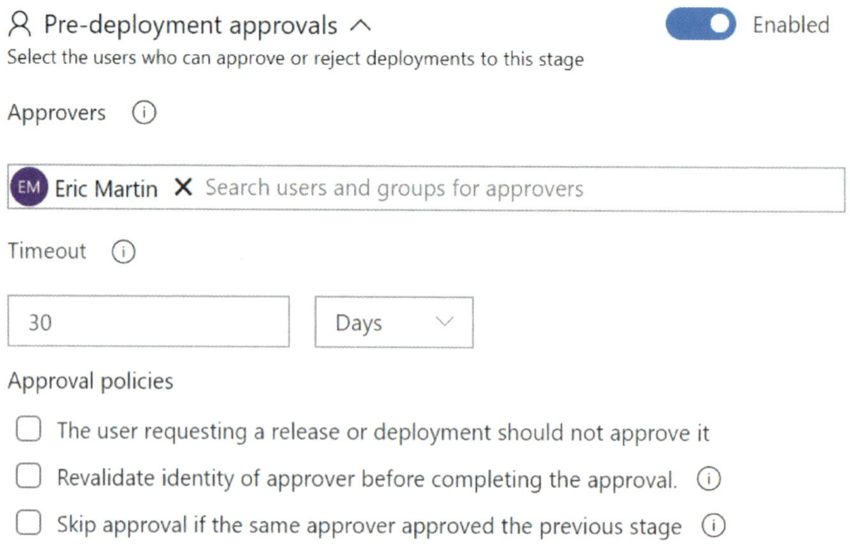

Figure 185: pre-deployment approval

Under the triggers section, you have the possibility to schedule the release. For example, if you want your releases to automatically be deployed on a Tuesday at 23:00 local time, then you can set it as below.

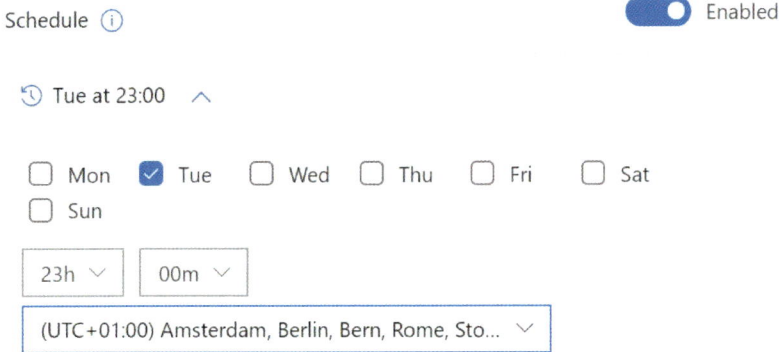

Figure 186: Schedule the production release

Even after the release, you can take some actions. For example, you might want to do things like checking if there are any alerts from the deployed environment after the deployment. As we are using Azure to deploy our application, we can add a gate to check for any Azure Monitor alerts as shown in Figure 187.

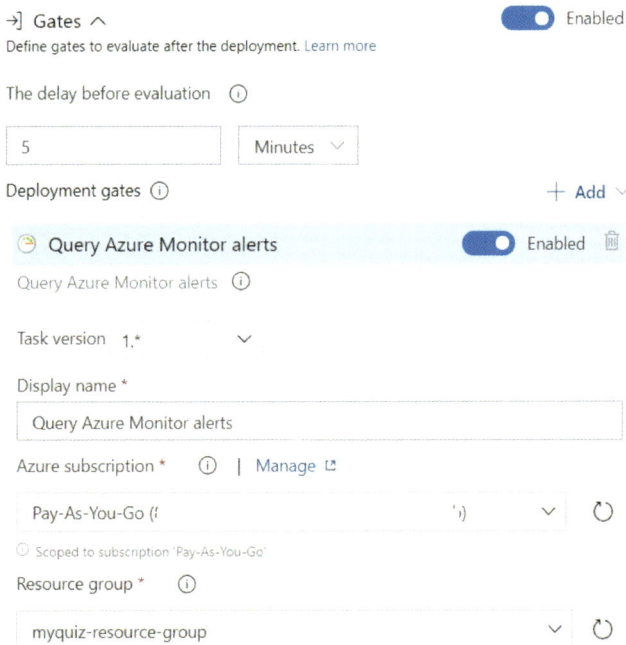

Figure 187: Query Azure monitor alerts using Gates

Create a release and try to check all the conditions. You will see windows like the following where things need to be approved.

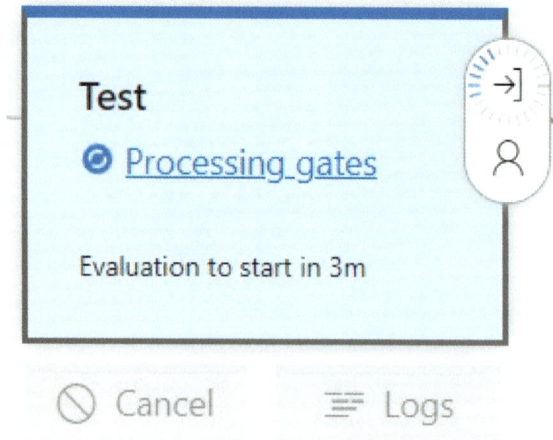

Figure 188: Waiting for approvals and gate checks

In this way, you have full control over your release process and automating makes your life easier as a developer, release manager or any other involved in the process. In other words, the whole organization develops a DevOps culture that will unite people, processes and products which allows continuous delivery of high-quality value to your customers.

Summary

In this chapter about Azure Pipelines, you learned the most vital section in the DevOps process. You created a build pipeline that builds your application on a build agent. We used yaml as a data serialization language to define the build definition. Then you created a release pipeline that is used to take the output of the build pipeline as an input and deploy it to various environments such as dev, test and production. Approvals, triggers and gates help us to have control over the full release process.

Index

Bibliography

[1] What is Azure DevOps - https://azure.microsoft.com/en-us/overview/what-is-devops/

[2] Definition of Scrum - https://www.scrumguides.org/scrum-guide.html#definition

[3] Adopt a Git branching strategy

https://docs.microsoft.com/en-us/azure/devops/repos/git/git-branching-guidance?view=azure-devops

[4] Azure DevOps Home page - https://azure.microsoft.com/en-us/services/devops/?nav=min

[5] Choose a process - https://docs.microsoft.com/en-us/azure/devops/boards/work-items/guidance/choose-process?view=azure-devops&tabs=basic-process

Printed in Great Britain
by Amazon

78147619R00105